PIZZA
NIGHT

KATE McMILLAN

PHOTOGRAPHS BY ERIN KUNKEL

weldon**owen**

CONTENTS

PIZZA FOR DINNER

Everyone likes pizza night. And if there's anything better than pizza night, it's homemade pizza night. Making pizza at home that is the equal of some of the best pies you have tasted in pizzerias is surprisingly easy. Indeed, all that's needed for even the novice cook to master pizza making at home is a little planning, a few hours of practice, and a collection of great recipes.

With this book in hand, you can gather family and friends for a pizza dinner whenever the inspiration or the craving strikes. Here, you'll find simple recipes for doughs, sauces, pizzas, salads, and sides, as well as tips and timelines for ensuring that pizza night is a delicious, wholesome, and fun meal everyone will enjoy.

One reason pizza is wildly popular is because it boasts countless variations. For example, a crust can be gluten-free or whole wheat, cracker thin or deep dish. It might be spread with a traditional tomato sauce or with a heady basil pesto and then topped with nearly any cheese imaginable, from mozzarella to ricotta to feta, along with a vegetable, meat, or seafood. It is easily geared to dietary restrictions, too, whether diners are vegetarians, gluten intolerant, or just watching calories.

Doughs and sauces can often be made in advance and frozen, a time-saver for busy cooks. Toward that end, each of the dough recipes that follows yields two crusts, so you can use half of the dough the day you make it and freeze the rest for another night. With the dough and sauce already on hand, a whole pie can come together in less than a half hour. When you pair it with an easy vegetable-based side dish, pizza night becomes a balanced dinner.

Making your own pizza also saves money, and you can control the quality of the ingredients and what and how much goes on each pie. Pizza night might feature a classic offering, such as a margherita, or be an excuse to use up leftovers in the fridge, like cooked chicken or last night's grilled zucchini. For weekend entertaining, it's easy to dress up pizza with special toppings. You might even arrange the options on a buffet and invite guests to assemble their own pies.

Once you dip into the following pages, impatiently awaiting a pizza delivery or sliding a supermarket-bought frozen pie into the oven will be forever in the past, and pizza night will mean only one thing: pizza made just the way everyone likes it.

ANATOMY OF A PIZZA

A classic pizza consists of four components: the base, the sauce, the toppings, and the garnishes. Each component offers a number of possibilities, so that you can customize each pie to your liking. You can even leave out one or more of the components, depending on the combination you choose. Here are a few tips to ensure that what you select for each component will add up to a successful pizza.

THE BASE

The base must be sturdy enough to stand up to your chosen toppings and complement their flavors. Each recipe offers a suggested base, but feel free to opt for what works best for you.

THE SAUCE

The choice of sauce helps inform what your toppings will be. Spread the sauce on the base with a light touch. It should act as a seasoning for the pizza, bringing all the elements together.

THE TOPPINGS

Never pile on too many toppings, in either number or weight. A few carefully selected ingredients will ensure that each one will shine. Use cheese prudently, so it doesn't overwhelm the flavors of the other ingredients.

THE GARNISHES

Employ simplicity for garnishes, such as a sprinkle of coarse salt to enhance all of the flavors, a drizzle of olive oil for an attractive sheen, a scattering of red pepper flakes for a touch of heat, or a small handful of torn herbs for a bright, fresh finish.

PIZZA PRIMER

Making pizza at home is easy and doesn't need to be time-consuming or labor-intensive. With just a few tools, a little prep work, and some everyday skills, serving homemade slices is doable on any weeknight schedule. Keep these tips and tricks in mind and you'll make a terrific pizza every time.

FOOLPROOF PIZZA FORMULA

You don't need to learn to toss pizza dough in the air to become a pizza pro. In fact, just a little practice goes a long way in perfecting your pies. Here's a formula to guide you on your way to flavorful pizzas with crispy crusts and bubbly-cheese perfection.

FRESH IS BEST Starting with top-notch ingredients is the best way to guarantee tasty results. Buy the best-quality cheese, olive oil, and toppings your budget will allow.

LET IT REST If your dough continues to bounce back when you are stretching it out, set it aside to rest for a few minutes, then try again.

LEAVE AN INCH Leave at least a 1-inch (2.5-cm) border of bare crust (brushed with olive oil), so the toppings won't escape over the edges during baking.

LESS IS MORE To avoid overtopping a pizza, which can yield a gummy crust and floppy slices, approach your toppings with the "less is more" rule. First, lightly coat all but the 1-inch (2.5-cm) border of the crust with the sauce. Next, apply the cheese so that it barely covers just the sauce. For toppings, keep it simple, using no more than three and scattering them lightly enough that the cheese is still visible.

HEAT IT UP Before baking a pizza, make sure the oven has reached its highest possible temperature and that the pizza stone has had time to absorb the heat. If the temperature is too low, the pizza will be undercooked. Resist the temptation to open the oven before the suggested cooking time has been reached.

TRANSFER WITH CARE The thought of transferring a pizza from a peel to a stone can be intimidating. To ensure success, make sure the peel is well floured before you top it with the pizza. If it isn't, when you try to slide the pizza onto the stone, the pizza will stick and toppings will go flying. Use a large, flat spatula first to loosen the pizza from the peel and then to guide it into the oven and onto the stone.

COOL, THEN CUT Once the pizza is out of the oven, let it cool for a few minutes before cutting. This will prevent burned mouths and will keep the melted cheese and toppings from sliding off the slices.

TOOLS FOR SUCCESS

These basic tools will help you craft a perfect pizza every time.

FOOD PROCESSOR This appliance makes quick work of mixing pizza dough, saving time and elbow grease.

PIZZA STONE Pizzas are baked on this flat piece of unglazed stoneware, which absorbs the high heat of the oven, producing a crisp crust.

PIZZA PEEL A wide paddle attached to a long handle, this tool helps simplify transferring a pizza to and from a hot oven.

PASTRY BRUSH This everyday kitchen tool is handy for brushing the edge of a pizza crust with olive oil just before baking.

CHEF'S KNIFE, KITCHEN SHEARS, OR A PIZZA WHEEL A large chef's knife is the best choice for cutting a pizza, though a pizza wheel or kitchen shears will also do the job.

BRINGING IT ALL TOGETHER

Making pizza is doable any day of the week, even on weeknights. Having your ingredients prepped and ready to go will ensure a smooth and efficient process. Before starting the dough, measure all the ingredients for it. When you're ready to assemble the first pie, have the sauce prepared, the cheeses and toppings cut as directed, and any necessary tools nearby.

PIZZA TIMELINE

UP TO A FEW WEEKS BEFORE (optional) Make and freeze the dough and sauce.

1-2 DAYS BEFORE Make (or thaw) the dough and sauce.

THE NIGHT BEFORE Shape the crust; prep the toppings (slice or grate cheeses; cook vegetable and protein toppings).

45 MINUTES BEFORE Preheat the oven and set out the sauce and toppings.

30 MINUTES BEFORE Add the sauce and toppings to the crust.

15 MINUTES BEFORE While the pizza bakes, assemble any side dishes.

5 MINUTES BEFORE Let the pizza cool.

DINNER IS SERVED! Cut and serve the pizza.

SHORTCUTS FOR A BUSY DAY

Use these shortcuts to get dinner on the table quickly and easily:

DOUGH Make and freeze homemade dough ahead of time, then thaw overnight in the refrigerator. Or, purchase premade dough at the grocery store or a local pizzeria.

SAUCE Buy jarred tomato sauce, or, for better flavor, pick up fresh pesto and other sauces at a deli counter or specialty food store.

TOPPINGS Head to the deli counter for easy toppings, such as cooked or cured meats, olives, and roasted vegetables.

SIDES & SALADS Toss fresh greens, such as arugula or baby kale, with olive oil and vinegar for an easy side dish. Or, purchase your favorite salad from the local deli or the prepared foods section of the grocery store.

WEEKEND PIZZA PARTY

For a crowd-friendly party idea, set up a toppings bar and invite guests to customize their own pies.

MAKE THE DOUGH IN ADVANCE Make multiple batches of dough, so that each guest has a ball of dough.

MAKE 1-3 SAUCES IN ADVANCE Tomato (page 26) and pesto (page 29) are classic crowd-pleasers.

SET UP A TOPPINGS BAR Put a variety of toppings—cheeses, meats, olives, vegetables, fresh herbs—in separate bowls for guests to pick and choose.

PREHEAT THE OVEN Before the guests arrive, place the pizza stone in the oven and crank up the heat to high.

CASUAL SERVING STYLE Encourage guests to make crusts in different shapes and to add their favorite toppings. Let them eat their pizzas soon after they come out of the oven. This is not the time for a sit-down dinner!

DOUGHS

3⅓ cups (17 oz/530 g) all-purpose flour, plus extra for dusting

¼ cup (1½ oz/45 g) whole-wheat flour

1 package (2½ teaspoons) quick-rise yeast

1 tablespoon sugar

1 tablespoon kosher salt

1¼ cups (10 fl oz/310 ml) warm water (110°F/43°C), plus extra as needed

2 tablespoon olive oil, plus extra as needed

THIN-CRUST PIZZA DOUGH

In a food processor, combine the flours, yeast, sugar, and salt. Pulse to mix the ingredients. With the motor running, add the water and olive oil in a steady stream, and then pulse until the dough comes together in a rough mass, about 12 seconds. If the dough does not form into a ball, sprinkle with 1–2 teaspoons of water and pulse again until a rough mass forms. Let the dough rest for 5–10 minutes.

Process the dough again for 25–30 seconds, steadying the top of the food processor with one hand. The dough should be tacky to the touch but not sticky. Transfer the dough to a lightly floured work surface and form into a smooth ball. Place the dough in a large oiled bowl, turn to coat with oil, and cover with plastic wrap. Let the dough rise in a warm place until doubled in bulk and spongy, about 1½ hours.

Turn the dough out onto a lightly floured work surface, punch it down, and shape into a smooth cylinder. Divide into 2 equal pieces. Shape each piece into a smooth ball, dusting with flour only if the dough becomes sticky. Cover both balls of dough with a clean kitchen towel and let rest for 10 minutes before proceeding with the pizza recipe of your choice. If you are using only one ball of dough, place the second ball in a gallon-size zipper-lock bag and freeze for up to 2 months. (When ready to use, thaw the frozen dough for 3–4 hours at room temperature.)

MAKES 2 BALLS OF DOUGH

ADD HERBS

To turn this classic dough into a crust that's flecked and flavored, just stir about 2 tablespoons chopped fresh herbs or 1 tablespoon crumbled dried herbs into the dry ingredients. Top picks for fragrant, crust-friendly results: oregano, thyme, basil, rosemary, sage, fennel seed, marjoram, or chives. Be wary of mixing too many flavors; try one or two herbs per recipe.

3¾ cups (19 oz/595 g) bread flour, plus extra for dusting

⅔ cup (3⅓ oz/100 g) medium-grind cornmeal

1½ tablespoons sugar

1 tablespoon kosher salt

1 package (2½ teaspoons) quick-rise yeast

1½ cups (12 fl oz/375 ml) warm water (110°F/43°C), plus extra as needed

5 tablespoons (3 fl oz/80 ml) olive oil, plus extra as needed

DEEP-DISH PIZZA DOUGH

The addition of cornmeal in this recipe creates a pleasing texture and an extra-savory taste. Originating in a pizzeria in Chicago, deep-dish pizza is made with a thick dough, so your finished pizza will more resemble a pie than a flatbread. One of the best pans for cooking a deep-dish pizza is a cast-iron skillet; the bottom and sides of the pan maintain a high temperature, producing a crispy crust.

In a food processor, combine the flour, cornmeal, sugar, salt, and yeast. Pulse to mix the ingredients. With the motor running, add the water and olive oil in a steady stream, then pulse until the dough comes together in a rough mass, about 12 seconds. If the dough does not form into a ball, sprinkle with 1–2 teaspoons of water and pulse again until a rough mass forms. Let rest for 5–10 minutes.

Process the dough again for 25–30 seconds, steadying the top of the food processor with one hand. The dough should be tacky to the touch but not sticky. Transfer the dough to a lightly floured work surface and form it into a smooth ball. Place the dough in a large oiled bowl, turn to coat with oil, and cover with plastic wrap. Let the dough rise in a warm place until doubled in bulk and spongy, about 2 hours.

Turn the dough out onto a lightly floured work surface, punch it down, and shape into a smooth cylinder. Divide the dough into 2 equal pieces. Shape each piece into a smooth ball, dusting with flour only if the dough becomes sticky. Cover both balls of dough with a clean kitchen towel and let rest for 10 minutes before proceeding with the pizza recipe of your choice. If you are using only one ball of dough, place the second ball in a gallon-size zipper-lock bag and freeze for up to 2 months. (When ready to use, thaw the frozen dough for 3–4 hours at room temperature.)

MAKES 2 BALLS OF DOUGH

2¾ cups (14 oz/440 g) gluten-free all-purpose flour mix, plus more for dusting

2 teaspoons sugar

1 teaspoon kosher salt, plus more for seasoning

¼ teaspoon baking soda

2 large eggs

¼ cup (2 fl oz/60 ml) extra-virgin olive oil, plus more for brushing

Freshly ground pepper

GLUTEN-FREE PIZZA DOUGH

In a large bowl, sift together the flour, sugar, salt, and baking soda. In a medium bowl, beat the eggs with the olive oil and ⅔ cup (5 fl oz/160 ml) water. Pour the egg mixture into the flour mixture. Using a fork, toss and stir until well combined.

Divide the dough into 2 equal pieces. Shape each piece into a smooth ball, dusting with flour only if the dough becomes sticky. Cover both balls of dough with a clean kitchen towel and let rest for 10 minutes before proceeding with the pizza recipe of your choice. If you are using only one ball of dough, place the second ball in a gallon-size zipper-lock bag and freeze for up to 2 months. (When ready to use, thaw the frozen dough for 3–4 hours at room temperature.)

MAKES 2 BALLS OF DOUGH

Because there is less elasticity in gluten-free pizza doughs, be careful not to stretch or roll the dough too thin, or it will tear. This recipe is a delicious foundation for pizza but too fragile for calzones and stromboli. Try adding 2 tablespoons chopped fresh thyme to add flecks of color and enticing scents.

2¼ cups (11½ oz/360 g) all-purpose flour, plus extra for dusting

1⅓ cups (7 oz/215 g) whole-wheat flour

1 package (2½ teaspoons) quick-rise yeast

2 teaspoons kosher salt

1 teaspoon sugar

1¼ cups (10 fl oz/310 ml) warm water (110°F/43°C), plus extra as needed

2 tablespoons olive oil, plus extra as needed

WHOLE-WHEAT PIZZA DOUGH

The secret to baking with whole-wheat flour is striking the perfect balance in a mixture of whole-wheat and all-purpose flours, so that the end result isn't too dense. This dough is nutty, flavorful, and bakes up with rustic, richly browned edges.

In a food processor, combine the flours, yeast, salt, and sugar. Pulse to mix the ingredients. With the motor running, add the water and olive oil in a steady stream, and then pulse until the dough comes together in a rough mass, about 12 seconds. If the dough does not form into a ball, sprinkle with 1–2 teaspoons of water and pulse again until a rough mass forms. Let rest for 5–10 minutes.

Process the dough again for 25–30 seconds, steadying the top of the food processor with one hand. The dough should be tacky to the touch but not sticky. Transfer the dough to a lightly floured work surface and form it into a smooth ball. Place the dough in a large oiled bowl, turn to coat with oil, and cover with plastic wrap. Let the dough rise in a warm place until doubled in bulk and spongy, about 1½ hours.

Turn the dough out onto a lightly floured work surface, punch it down, and knead into a smooth cylinder. Divide the dough into 2 equal pieces. Shape each piece into a smooth ball, dusting with flour only if the dough becomes sticky. Cover both balls of dough with a clean kitchen towel and let rest for 10 minutes before proceeding with your chosen pizza recipe. If you are using only one ball of dough, place the second ball in a gallon-size zipper-lock bag and freeze for up to 2 months. (When ready to use, thaw the frozen dough for 3–4 hours at room temperature.)

MAKES 2 BALLS OF DOUGH

1 head cauliflower, thick stems removed, cut into small florets

3 tablespoons almond flour

3 tablespoons grated Parmesan cheese

3 tablespoons shredded mozzarella cheese

1 tablespoon olive oil, plus more for brushing

1 teaspoon kosher salt

½ teaspoon dried basil

½ teaspoon garlic powder

1 large egg yolk

CAULIFLOWER PIZZA DOUGH

Place a pizza stone in the middle of the oven and preheat to 450°F (230°C). Once the oven has reached 450°F (230°C), let the stone continue to heat for 15–30 minutes longer, without opening the door.

Put the cauliflower in a food processor and pulse until the florets are evenly chopped into tiny snowflake-like pieces, about 30 pulses. Transfer to a microwave-safe bowl, cover the bowl with a paper towel, and microwave on high for 5 minutes. Pour the cauliflower onto a clean, dry kitchen towel. Using a wooden spoon, spread it out so that all of the steam can escape. Once cooled, wrap it in the towel tightly and squeeze out as much moisture as you can. It is imperative that you squeeze out as much moisture as you can or the crust will not hold together when you bake it.

Put the cauliflower in a bowl and add the almond flour, Parmesan, mozzarella, olive oil, salt, basil, garlic powder, and egg yolk. Stir well to combine. Cut a 12-inch (30-cm) piece of parchment paper, place it on a pizza peel, and brush it lightly with olive oil. Turn the dough out onto the oiled paper. Using your hands, form the dough into a 9-inch (23-cm) circle, pressing gently and making sure to keep the edges from cracking.

Carefully transfer the dough (keeping it on the parchment paper) onto the hot pizza stone in the oven and bake for 10 minutes. Using the peel, remove the dough from the oven. Leaving a 1-inch (2.5-cm) border, spread your desired sauce over the dough and top with your desired cheeses. Distribute your desired toppings evenly around the pizza. Return the pizza to the stone and bake for another 5 minutes. Transfer the pizza to a cutting board, let cool for a few minutes, then slice and serve.

MAKES 1 BALL OF DOUGH

Unlike wheat flour pizza bases, this dough needs to be partially baked before topping. A crust made of finely chopped cauliflower, cheese, and spices is an elegant gluten-free alternative to wheat flour crust—and a delicious way to add extra vegetables to your kids' diets. The key to success here is getting as much moisture out of the cauliflower as you can. Once you think you've drained it as much as possible, squeeze it in the towel a few more times.

SAUCES

¼ cup (2 fl oz/60 ml) olive oil

5 cloves garlic, minced

1 can (15 oz/470 g) crushed tomatoes

1 teaspoon dried basil

¾ teaspoon dried oregano

¼ teaspoon dried thyme

¼ teaspoon freshly ground pepper

1½–2 tablespoons red wine vinegar

Kosher salt

TOMATO SAUCE

——————>>>>>>>>>>

This recipe is as simple as it gets. A splash of red wine vinegar brightens all the flavors and brings them forward. Canned tomatoes make this sauce accessible throughout the year, and it freezes really well. Experiment with different herbs to marry the sauce to various toppings.

In a small frying pan over medium heat, warm the olive oil. Add the garlic and cook, stirring frequently, until fragrant, 1–2 minutes. Be careful not to let it scorch or the garlic will taste bitter.

In a bowl, stir together the garlic-oil mixture, tomatoes, dried basil, oregano, thyme, pepper, ⅓ cup (3 fl oz/80 ml) water, and 1½ tablespoons of the vinegar. Season to taste with salt and additional vinegar. Use right away or refrigerate in an airtight container for up to 1 week.

MAKES ABOUT 2¾ CUPS (22 OZ/690 G)

1 clove garlic, minced

2 oil-packed anchovies, rinsed

1½ cups (7½ oz/235 g) pitted brine-cured olives (black, green, or a mixture)

¼ cup (¼ oz/7 g) loosely packed fresh herb leaves such as thyme, oregano, or basil, or a mixture

Grated zest of 1 lemon

3 tablespoons olive oil

⅛ teaspoon red pepper flakes (optional)

OLIVE TAPENADE

In a food processor, combine the garlic and anchovies and pulse to mince. Add the olives, herbs, lemon zest, olive oil, and red pepper flakes, if using. Process until the texture is to your liking, either to a coarse or smooth purée.

Use right away, or store in an airtight container in the refrigerator for up to 2 weeks.

MAKES 1¼ CUPS (10 FL OZ/310 ML)

Olive tapenade matches perfectly to hot, crisp pizza dough. Choose the ingredients you put on top selectively—because olives are so salty, it's best to use a mild cheese and other ingredients that aren't naturally salty themselves. Leftover tapenade is terrific served with crostini and goat cheese.

2 tablespoons pine nuts

2½ cups (2½ oz/75 g) fresh basil leaves, packed

5 cloves garlic, minced

¾ cup (6 fl oz/180 ml) extra-virgin olive oil

⅛ teaspoon fine sea salt, plus more as needed

2 tablespoons grated Parmesan cheese

BASIL PESTO

To toast the pine nuts, in a small dry frying pan, warm the pine nuts over medium heat, shaking the pan occasionally, until fragrant and lightly browned, 2–3 minutes. Transfer the pine nuts to a plate and let cool to room temperature.

In a food processor, combine the toasted pine nuts, basil, garlic, olive oil, and sea salt. Process for about 30 seconds, scraping down the sides of the bowl once or twice. Add the cheese and process until combined, about 5 seconds more.

Season to taste with additional sea salt. Use right away or refrigerate in an airtight container for up to 2 days, or freeze in a freezer-safe container for up to 3 months.

MAKES 1 CUP (9 OZ/240 G)

A great pesto explodes with flavor, so you don't need many toppings to make a great pizza. Pesto freezes beautifully, and since a little goes a long way, freeze it in smaller portions to make weeknight cooking faster and easier (ice cube trays offer the perfect compartments).

2 tablespoons olive oil

½ yellow onion, minced

3 cloves garlic, minced

Kosher salt and freshly ground pepper

1 cup (8 oz/250 g) whole-milk ricotta cheese

¼ cup (2 fl oz/60 ml) heavy cream

1 tablespoon fresh oregano leaves, chopped

WHITE PIZZA SAUCE

>>>>>>>>>

This creamy sauce—made with ricotta, garlic, and fragrant oregano—is a great change up from red sauce. It makes a delicious base for pizza topped with roasted or grilled vegetables.

In a small frying pan over medium heat, warm the oil. Add the onion, garlic, and a pinch each of salt and pepper. Sauté until the onion is translucent, 3–4 minutes, taking care not to let the onion or garlic brown. Transfer the contents of the pan, including all of the oil, to a bowl and let cool.

When the onion mixture is cool, stir in the ricotta, cream, and oregano. Taste and season with more salt and pepper, if needed.

Use right away, or store in an airtight container in the refrigerator for up to 1 week. The white sauce can be frozen for up to 2 months.

MAKES 1¼ CUPS (10 FL OZ/310 ML)

2 red bell peppers

1 clove garlic, minced

½ cup (2 oz/60 g) walnuts halves or pieces, toasted and roughly chopped

¼ cup (1 oz/30 g) grated Parmesan cheese

3 tablespoons olive oil

Kosher salt and freshly ground pepper

ROASTED RED PEPPER PESTO

Using tongs or a large fork, hold 1 bell pepper at a time directly over the flame of a gas burner, or place directly on the grate. Roast, turning as needed, until blistered and charred black on all sides, 10–15 minutes total. (Alternatively, place the peppers under a preheated broiler, as close as possible to the heating element, and roast to char them on all sides, turning as needed.) Transfer the peppers to a bowl, cover with plastic wrap or a clean kitchen towel, and set aside to steam until cooled, about 20 minutes. Once cool, peel or rub away the charred skins, then seed the peppers and cut into chunks.

In a food processor or blender, combine the roasted peppers, garlic, walnuts, Parmesan, and olive oil. Process until smooth. Stop the machine and taste the pesto; adjust the seasoning with salt and pepper, pulsing to mix.

Use right away, or store in an airtight container in the refrigerator for up to 1 week. The pesto can be frozen for up to 2 months.

MAKES 1½ CUPS (12 FL OZ/375 ML)

An alternative to traditional basil pesto, red peppers and toasted walnuts make a flavorful and colorful pesto that works beautifully with both vegetable and meat toppings. Roasting your own bell peppers is a quick and easy task.

PIZZAS

vegetarian • meat • specialty

½ lb (250 g) asparagus, tough woody ends removed

2 teaspoons olive oil, plus more for brushing and drizzling

Kosher salt and freshly ground pepper

1 ball Thin-Crust Pizza Dough (page 17) or Whole-Wheat Pizza Dough (page 20)

1 recipe White Pizza Sauce (page 30)

4–6 fresh basil leaves, torn into large pieces

1 tablespoon fresh oregano leaves

1 large egg

SHAVED ASPARAGUS & HERB PIZZA WITH EGG

Place a pizza stone in the middle of the oven and preheat to 450°F (230°C). Once the oven has reached 450°F (230°C), let the stone continue to heat for 15–30 minutes longer, without opening the door.

Using a vegetable peeler, shave the asparagus spears into long, thin ribbons. Transfer to a bowl, toss with the olive oil, and season with salt and pepper. Set aside.

On a floured pizza peel, stretch or roll out the pizza dough into a 12-inch (30-cm) round. If the dough springs back, let it rest for about 10 minutes before continuing. Brush the entire dough round with olive oil and season lightly with salt and pepper. Leaving a 1-inch (2.5-cm) border, spread the sauce over the dough. Arrange the asparagus ribbons attractively on the pizza and scatter the basil and oregano all over the top. Drizzle with a little more olive oil.

Carefully slide the pizza from the peel onto the hot stone in the oven and bake until the crust begins to brown, about 6 minutes. Crack the egg into a small bowl, being careful not to break the yolk. Open the oven door and quickly slide the egg from the bowl onto the center of the pizza. Continue baking until the egg is set but the yolk is still runny, 4–6 minutes longer.

Transfer the pizza to a cutting board. Let cool for a few minutes, then slice and serve right away.

SERVES 4

BREAKFAST FOR DINNER

Eggs on pizza may seem curious, but one taste and you'll be hooked. The warm yolk oozes into the sauce, adding creaminess and a savory farm-to-table complement to the ricotta-based sauce. The white color of the sauce also sets off the green of the asparagus, shaved into ribbons for flash roasting. You can divide the recipe into 4 individual pizzas and top each with an egg for a charming brunch dish.

1 ball Thin-Crust Pizza Dough (page 17) or Whole-Wheat Pizza Dough (page 20)

Olive oil for brushing and drizzling

Kosher salt and freshly ground pepper

1 cup (8 fl oz/250 ml) Tomato Sauce (page 26), or 3 ripe plum tomatoes, thinly sliced

8 oz (250 g) fresh mozzarella cheese, preferably buffalo, thinly sliced and torn into 1-inch (2.5-cm) pieces

Fresh basil leaves, for garnish

MARGHERITA PIZZA

MAKE IT CLASSIC

➤➤➤➤➤➤➤➤

Originating in the late 1800s in Naples to honor Queen Margherita, this pizza is commonly thought of as the one to measure all others by. It's best not to fuss around too much with this classic, and instead, let the 3 star ingredients stand out on their own.

Place a pizza stone in the middle of the oven and preheat to 450°F (230°C). Once the oven has reached 450°F (230°C), let the stone continue to heat for 15–30 minutes longer, without opening the door.

On a floured pizza peel, stretch or roll out the pizza dough into a 12-inch (30-cm) round. If the dough springs back, let it rest for about 10 minutes before continuing. Brush the entire dough round with olive oil and season with salt and pepper. Leaving a 1-inch (2.5-cm) border, spread the sauce over the dough (or distribute the tomato slices evenly around the pizza) and top with the cheese. Season again with salt and pepper.

Carefully slide the pizza from the peel onto the hot stone in the oven and bake for 10–12 minutes, or until the crust is golden brown. Using the peel, transfer the pizza to a cutting board, and drizzle with olive oil. Let cool for a few minutes, then scatter basil over the top, slice, and serve.

SERVES 4

4 tablespoons (2 fl oz/60 ml) olive oil, plus more for brushing

2 cloves garlic, minced

5 oz (155 g) wild mushrooms such as cremini, shiitake, or oyster or a mixture, brushed clean

Kosher salt and freshly ground pepper

5 oz (155 g) baby kale or stemmed (including tough center spines) and chopped regular kale

1 ball Thin-Crust Pizza Dough (page 17) or Whole-Wheat Pizza Dough (page 20)

1 cup (8 fl oz/250 ml) Tomato Sauce (page 26)

1½ cups (6 oz/185 g) shredded fontina cheese

WILD MUSHROOM, KALE & FONTINA PIZZA

Place a pizza stone in the middle of the oven and preheat to 450°F (230°C). Once the oven has reached 450°F (230°C), let the stone continue to heat for 15–30 minutes longer, without opening the door.

In a frying pan over medium-high heat, warm 3 tablespoons of the olive oil. Add the garlic and sauté just until it begins to soften but not brown, about 1 minute. Then add the mushrooms, season with salt and pepper, and sauté until soft, about 4 minutes. Add the remaining 1 tablespoon olive oil and the kale and stir to coat the kale with the oil. Sauté just until the kale begins to wilt, about 2 minutes. Taste and adjust the seasoning. Remove from the heat and set aside.

On a floured pizza peel, stretch or roll out the pizza dough into a 12-inch (30-cm) round. If the dough springs back, let it rest for about 10 minutes before continuing. Leaving a 1-inch (2.5-cm) border, spread the sauce over the dough round and top with the cheese. Distribute the mushroom and kale mixture evenly around the pizza. Brush the outside edge of the dough with olive oil and season the whole pizza lightly with salt and pepper.

Carefully slide the pizza from the peel onto the hot stone in the oven and bake for 10–12 minutes, or until the crust is golden brown. Using the peel, transfer the pizza to a cutting board. Let cool for a few minutes, then slice and serve right away.

SERVES 4

To make a square pizza, shape the dough to fit a 12-inch (30-cm) rimmed baking sheet. A baking sheet can act in place of a pizza stone since it too can handle high temperatures and absorb heat. Your pizza may come out less crunchy in a baking sheet than on a pizza stone. You can also place a baking sheet on a preheated pizza stone for best results.

1 tablespoon olive oil

1 bunch spinach, thick stems removed, washed and thoroughly dried

Kosher salt and freshly ground pepper

1 ball Thin-Crust Pizza Dough (page 17) or Whole-Wheat Pizza Dough (page 20)

¾ cup (6 fl oz/180 ml) Olive Tapenade (page 27)

1 cup (4 oz/125 g) shredded low-moisture mozzarella cheese

1 can (14 oz/440 g) artichoke hearts, drained thoroughly and quartered

½ cup (3 oz/90 g) cherry or grape tomatoes, halved

ARTICHOKE, SPINACH & OLIVE TAPENADE PIZZA

MEATLESS MONDAY

→→→→→→→→→

Here, fresh Mediterranean flavors combine for a delicious vegetarian pizza. Simply drain the artichokes and quickly sauté the spinach, and dinner is halfway done. Full of fresh, flavorful vegetables, this is a perfect pizza for a Meatless Monday.

Place a pizza stone in the middle of the oven and preheat to 450°F (230°C). Once the oven has reached 450°F (230°C), let the stone continue to heat for 15–30 minutes longer, without opening the door.

Warm the olive oil in a frying pan over medium-high heat. Add the spinach and season with salt and pepper. Sauté just until the spinach is mostly wilted, about 2 minutes. Remove from the heat and let cool for a few minutes. Drain the cooked spinach thoroughly to prevent a soggy pizza. Set aside.

On a floured pizza peel, stretch or roll out the pizza dough into a 12-inch (30-cm) round. If the dough springs back, let it rest for about 10 minutes before continuing. Leaving a 1-inch (2.5-cm) border, spread the tapenade over the dough round and top with the cheese. Distribute the spinach, artichoke hearts, and tomato halves evenly around the pizza. Brush the outside edge of the dough with olive oil and season the whole pizza lightly with salt and pepper.

Carefully slide the pizza from the peel onto the hot stone in the oven and bake for 10–12 minutes, or until the crust is golden brown. Using the peel, transfer the pizza to a cutting board. Let cool for a few minutes, then slice and serve right away.

SERVES 4

1 large eggplant, about 1 lb (500 g), cut into ½-inch (12-mm) dice

5 tablespoons (3 fl oz/80 ml) olive oil, plus more for brushing

Kosher salt and freshly ground black pepper

1 ball Thin-Crust Pizza Dough (page 17) or Whole-Wheat Pizza Dough (page 20)

1 cup (8 fl oz/250 ml) Tomato Sauce (page 26)

¾ teaspoon red pepper flakes

10 oz (315 g) fresh mozzarella cheese, preferably buffalo, thinly sliced and torn into 1-inch (2.5-cm) pieces

½ cup (3 oz/90 g) cherry tomatoes, halved

6–8 fresh basil leaves, torn into big pieces

SPICY EGGPLANT, BASIL & TOMATO PIZZA

Place a pizza stone on the bottom rack of the oven and preheat to 400°F (200°C). (This way your pizza stone will get very hot while you are roasting the eggplant.)

Pile the eggplant on a baking sheet lined with parchment paper. Drizzle with the olive oil, season well with salt and black pepper, and toss to coat. Spread the eggplant in a single layer and roast in the middle of the oven, stirring once about halfway through, until fork-tender, about 25 minutes. Remove from the oven and set aside.

Raise the oven temperature to 450°F (230°C). Wearing oven mitts, carefully move the pizza stone to the upper rack of the oven.

On a floured pizza peel, stretch or roll out the pizza dough into a 12-inch (30-cm) round. If the dough springs back, let it rest for about 10 minutes before continuing. Leaving a 1-inch (2.5-cm) border, spread the sauce over the dough round and sprinkle with the red pepper flakes. Top with the eggplant, cheese, and tomato halves, distributing them evenly around the pizza. Brush the outside edge of the dough with olive oil and season the whole pizza lightly with salt and black pepper.

Carefully slide the pizza from the peel onto the hot stone in the oven and bake for 10–12 minutes, or until the crust is golden brown. Using the peel, transfer the pizza to a cutting board and scatter the basil all over the top. Let cool for a few minutes, then slice and serve right away.

SERVES 4

VEGGIE NIGHT

━◄◄◄◄◄◄◄◄━━

Roasting the eggplant first transforms it into a sweet and tender topping that melts into the cheese. For a milder pizza, omit the red pepper flakes and pass them at the table for those that like a little spice.

2 large leeks, white and tender green parts only

3 small red-skinned potatoes

2 tablespoons olive oil, plus more for brushing

Kosher salt and freshly ground pepper

1 ball Thin-Crust Pizza Dough (page 17) or Whole-Wheat Pizza Dough (page 20)

1 cup (8 fl oz/250 ml) White Pizza Sauce (page 30)

2 tablespoons fresh rosemary leaves, minced

LEEK, POTATO & ROSEMARY PIZZA

SPECIAL NIGHT

————▸▸▸▸▸▸▸▸▸————

The high temperature of the oven renders the red-tipped slices of potato golden and crispy. Here, they meld with a combination of sweet caramelized leeks, fresh rosemary, and creamy cheese sauce for an indulgent treat.

Place a pizza stone in the middle of the oven and preheat to 450°F (230°C). Once the oven has reached 450°F (230°C), let the stone continue to heat for 15–30 minutes longer, without opening the door.

Cut the trimmed leeks in half lengthwise, then slice crosswise. Rinse thoroughly in a colander or salad spinner, then drain well and pat or spin dry thoroughly. Set aside. Using a sharp chef's knife or a mandoline, cut the potatoes into paper-thin slices. Set aside.

Warm the olive oil in a frying pan over medium heat. Add the leeks and season with salt and pepper. Sauté until soft, about 6 minutes. Remove from the heat and set aside.

On a floured pizza peel, stretch or roll out the pizza dough into a 12-inch (30-cm) round. If the dough springs back, let it rest for about 10 minutes before continuing. Leaving a 1-inch (2.5-cm) border, spread the sauce over the dough round. Cover the sauce with the potato slices, overlapping them slightly. Top with the leeks, including all the oil from the pan, and sprinkle with the rosemary. Brush the outside edge of the dough with olive oil and season the whole pizza lightly with salt and pepper.

Carefully slide the pizza from the peel onto the hot stone in the oven and bake for 10–12 minutes, or until the crust is golden brown. Using the peel, transfer the pizza to a cutting board. Let cool for a few minutes, then slice and serve right away.

SERVES 4

1 small bunch broccoli rabe, thick stems removed

2 tablespoons olive oil, plus more for brushing

6 cloves garlic, thinly sliced

¼ teaspoon red pepper flakes, or to taste

Kosher salt and freshly ground black pepper

Juice of ½ lemon

1 ball Thin-Crust Pizza Dough (page 17) or Whole-Wheat Pizza Dough (page 20)

1 cup (8 fl oz/250 ml) Tomato Sauce (page 26)

2 cups (8 oz/250 g) shredded smoked mozzarella cheese

BROCCOLI RABE, GARLIC & SMOKED MOZZARELLA PIZZA

Place a pizza stone in the middle of the oven and preheat to 450°F (230°C). Once the oven has reached 450°F (230°C), let the stone continue to heat for 15–30 minutes longer, without opening the door.

Bring a saucepan of water to a boil over high heat. Add the broccoli rabe and cook until the stems are tender-crisp, about 3 minutes. Drain well and let cool. When cool enough to handle, cut into 2-inch (5-cm) pieces. Set aside.

Warm the olive oil in a frying pan over medium-high heat. Add the garlic and red pepper flakes and sauté just until the garlic begins to soften but not brown, about 1 minute. Add the chopped broccoli rabe and stir to coat each piece with the oil. Season to taste with salt and black pepper and stir in the lemon juice. Remove from the heat and set aside.

On a floured pizza peel, stretch or roll out the pizza dough into a 12-inch (30-cm) round. If the dough springs back, let it rest for about 10 minutes before continuing. Leaving a 1-inch (2.5-cm) border, spread the sauce over the dough round and top with the cheese. Distribute the broccoli rabe evenly around the pizza. Brush the outside edge of the dough with olive oil and season the whole pizza lightly with salt and black pepper.

Carefully slide the pizza from the peel onto the hot stone in the oven and bake for 10–12 minutes, or until the crust is golden brown. Using the peel, transfer the pizza to a cutting board. Let cool for a few minutes, then slice and serve right away.

SERVES 4

When topped on a scrumptious pizza, vegetables become infinitely more appealing. Here nutrient-rich broccoli rabe is first boiled, then sautéed with garlic, red pepper, and oil, to ensure the tenderest and most flavorful vegetable. If picky eaters are still reluctant to dive in, dust the entire pizza in a light coating of Parmesan cheese.

1 ball Thin-Crust Pizza Dough (page 17) or Whole-Wheat Pizza Dough (page 20)

1 cup (8 fl oz/250 ml) Tomato Sauce (page 26)

4–6 fresh basil leaves, torn into big pieces

4 oz (125 g) fresh mozzarella cheese, preferably buffalo, thinly sliced

½ cup (2½ oz/75 g) crumbled Gorgonzola cheese

⅓ cup (2½ oz/75 g) whole-milk ricotta cheese

¼ cup (1 oz/30 g) grated Parmesan cheese

Olive oil for brushing

Kosher salt and freshly ground pepper

FOUR CHEESE PIZZA

CHOOSE YOUR CHEESE

"Quattro formaggi" pizza is a timeless tradition in Italy—but which four cheeses you use is up for discussion. Three of them are standard: mozzarella, Parmesan, and ricotta. This recipe uses an assertive gorgonzola for the fourth, but you can choose from any number of cheeses, from mild to extra-sharp, such as fontina, smoked mozzarella, or pecorino.

Place a pizza stone in the middle of the oven and preheat to 450°F (230°C). Once the oven has reached 450°F (230°C), let the stone continue to heat for 15–30 minutes longer, without opening the door.

On a floured pizza peel, stretch or roll out the pizza dough into a 12-inch (30-cm) round. If the dough springs back, let it rest for about 10 minutes before continuing. Leaving a 1-inch (2.5-cm) border, spread the sauce over the dough round and top with the basil and all of the cheeses. Brush the outside edge of the dough with olive oil and season the whole pizza lightly with salt and pepper.

Carefully slide the pizza from the peel onto the hot stone in the oven and bake for 10–12 minutes, or until the crust is golden brown. Using the peel, transfer the pizza to a cutting board. Let cool for a few minutes, then slice and serve right away.

SERVES 4

1 tablespoon olive oil, plus more for brushing

1 clove garlic, minced

2 small zucchini, about ½ lb (250 g) total weight, cut in half lengthwise and sliced crosswise into ¼-inch (6-mm) half-moons

1 red bell pepper, seeded and diced

Kosher salt and freshly ground pepper

1 ball Thin-Crust Pizza Dough (page 17) or Whole-Wheat Pizza Dough (page 20)

1 cup (8 fl oz/250 ml) Tomato Sauce (page 26)

½ cup (2 oz/60 g) shredded low-moisture mozzarella cheese

8 oz (250 g) teleme cheese, cut into small dice

⅓ cup (2 oz/60 g) brine-cured black olives, pitted and halved lengthwise

ZUCCHINI, RED PEPPER, OLIVE & TELEME PIZZA

Place a pizza stone in the middle of the oven and preheat to 450°F (230°C). Once the oven has reached 450°F (230°C), let the stone continue to heat for 15–30 minutes longer, without opening the door.

Warm the olive oil in a frying pan over medium-high heat. Add the garlic and sauté just until it begins to soften but not brown, about 1 minute. Add the zucchini and bell pepper, season well with salt and pepper, and sauté until the vegetables are fork-tender, about 5 minutes. Remove from the heat and set aside.

On a floured pizza peel, stretch or roll out the pizza dough into a 12-inch (30-cm) round. If the dough springs back, let it rest for about 10 minutes before continuing. Leaving a 1-inch (2.5-cm) border, spread the sauce over the dough round and top with the cheeses. Distribute the zucchini and bell pepper mixture and the olives evenly around the pizza. Brush the outside edge of the dough with olive oil and season the whole pizza lightly with salt and pepper.

Carefully slide the pizza from the peel onto the hot stone in the oven and bake for 10–12 minutes, or until the crust is golden brown. Using the peel, transfer the pizza to a cutting board. Let cool for a few minutes, then slice and serve right away.

SERVES 4

SUMMER PIZZA NIGHT

Since the baking time for an assembled pizza is so short, some toppings, like these featured here, need to be cooked in advance. Teleme cheese, originally from the San Francisco Bay Area, has a creamy texture similar to brie.

1 ball Thin-Crust Pizza Dough (page 17) or Whole-Wheat Pizza Dough (page 20)

Olive oil for brushing and drizzling

Freshly ground pepper

1 cup (8 fl oz/250 ml) Olive Tapenade (page 27)

1½ cups (7 ½ oz/235 g) crumbled feta cheese

1½ cups (9 oz/280 g) cherry tomatoes, preferably a mixture of colors, halved

6–8 fresh basil leaves, julienned

FETA, CHERRY TOMATO & OLIVE TAPENADE PIZZETTES

MEDITERRANEAN NIGHT

——▸▸▸▸▸▸▸▸

This eye-catching and colorful pizza gets a good amount of saltiness from both the feta and the rich olive tapenade sauce, which is balanced by tart tomatoes and fragrant basil. Serve with a Chopped Salad (page 107) and a lively red wine.

Place a pizza stone in the middle of the oven and preheat to 450°F (230°C). Once the oven has reached 450°F (230°C), let the stone continue to heat for 15–30 minutes longer, without opening the door.

Divide the pizza dough into 8 equal pieces. On a floured pizza peel, roll out each piece into a 5-inch (13-cm) round. If the dough springs back, let it rest for about 10 minutes before continuing. Brush each dough round with olive oil and season with pepper. Leaving a 1-inch (2.5-cm) border, spread the tapenade over each dough round and top with the feta and tomato halves.

Carefully slide the pizzettes from the peel onto the hot stone in the oven and bake for 10–12 minutes, or until the crust is golden brown. Using the peel, transfer the pizzettes to a cutting board. Drizzle the finished pizzettes with olive oil. Let cool for a few minutes, then scatter the basil over the top and serve right away.

SERVES 4

1 large butternut squash, about 1½ lb (750 g), peeled, seeded, and cubed (about 3 cups/ 14¾ oz/420 g)

2 tablespoons olive oil, plus more for brushing

Kosher salt and freshly ground pepper

1 ball Thin-Crust Pizza Dough (page 17) or Whole-Wheat Pizza Dough (page 20)

1½ cups (6 oz/185 g) shredded smoked mozzarella cheese

8 fresh sage leaves

ROASTED SQUASH, SMOKED MOZZARELLA & SAGE PIZZETTES

Place a pizza stone on the bottom rack of the oven and preheat to 450°F (230°C). (This way your pizza stone will get very hot while you are roasting the squash.)

Pile the squash on a baking sheet lined with parchment paper. Drizzle with the olive oil, season well with salt and pepper, and toss to coat. Spread the squash out in a single layer and roast in the upper third of the oven, stirring once, until very soft and caramelized, about 30 minutes. Remove from the oven and set aside.

Wearing oven mitts, carefully move the pizza stone to the upper rack of the oven.

Divide the pizza dough into 8 equal pieces. On a floured pizza peel, roll out each piece into a 5-inch (13-cm) round. If the dough springs back, let it rest for about 10 minutes before continuing. Brush each dough round with olive oil and season with salt and pepper. Leaving a 1-inch (2.5-cm) border, distribute the cheese and then the butternut squash evenly over each pizzette. Place a sage leaf in the center of each pizzette.

Carefully slide the pizzettes from the peel onto the hot stone in the oven and bake for 10–12 minutes, or until the crust is golden brown. Using the peel, transfer the pizzettes to a cutting board. Let cool for a few minutes, then serve right away.

SERVES 4

MAKE IT SPECIAL

Butternut squash—sweet, dense and rich—and earthy sage is one of those culinary marriages that seems like destiny. The smoky mozzarella is another perfect match. For a full meal, serve with a crisp white wine and a Spinach, Pear, Red Onion & Bacon Salad (page 113).

½ lb (250 g) asparagus, tough woody ends removed

2 teaspoons olive oil, plus more for brushing and drizzling

Kosher salt and freshly ground pepper

1 ball Thin-Crust Pizza Dough (page 17) or Whole-Wheat Pizza Dough (page 20)

¾ cup (6 fl oz/180 ml) Roasted Red Pepper Pesto (page 31)

½ cup (2 oz/60 g) shredded low-moisture mozzarella cheese

5 oz (155 g) cold goat cheese

ASPARAGUS & GOAT CHEESE PIZZA WITH RED PEPPER PESTO

SPRINGTIME PIZZA

>>>>>>>>>

The roasted red pepper sauce adds a distinctly Italian flair to this pizza. You can swap in other vegetables for the asparagus, like tomatoes, spinach, and eggplant throughout the year. For a unique presentation, think outside of the typical triangle slices and try slicing into strips, rectangles, and squares.

Place a pizza stone in the middle of the oven and preheat to 450°F (230°C). Once the oven has reached 450°F (230°C), let the stone continue heat for 15–30 minutes longer, without opening the door.

Bring a saucepan of water to a boil over high heat. Add the asparagus and cook just until beginning to soften, 1–2 minutes. Drain and toss in a bowl with the olive oil and salt and pepper to taste.

On a floured pizza peel, stretch or roll out the pizza dough into a 12-inch (30-cm) oval, with even thickness across the oval. If the dough springs back, let it rest for about 10 minutes before continuing. Leaving a 1-inch (2.5-cm) border, spread the pesto over the dough and top with the mozzarella. Using your hands, crumble the goat cheese and distribute it evenly around the pizza. Arrange the asparagus spears horizontally with the dough. Brush the outside edge of the dough with olive oil and season the whole pizza lightly with salt and pepper.

Carefully slide the pizza from the peel onto the hot stone in the oven and bake for 10–12 minutes, or until the crust is golden brown. Using the peel, transfer the pizza to a cutting board. Drizzle with a little more olive oil. Let cool for a few minutes, then slice and serve right away.

SERVES 4

1 ball Thin-Crust Pizza Dough (page 17) or Whole-Wheat Pizza Dough (page 20)

1 cup (8 fl oz/250 ml) Basil Pesto (page 29)

¾ cup (6 oz/185 g) whole-milk ricotta cheese

1 cup (6 oz/185 g) cherry tomatoes, halved

3 tablespoons grated Parmesan cheese

Olive oil for brushing

Kosher salt and freshly ground pepper

4–6 fresh basil leaves, torn into large pieces

PESTO, RICOTTA & CHERRY TOMATO PIZZA

CLASSIC PIZZA NIGHT

>>>>>>>>>

This pizza strikes a delicious balance of creamy cheese, juicy tomatoes, and aromatic herbs. You could also use Roasted Red Pepper Pesto (page 31) for a sweeter flavor, or Olive Tapenade (page 27), which melts into succulence with the ricotta.

Place a pizza stone in the middle of the oven and preheat to 450°F (230°C). Once the oven has reached 450°F (230°C), let the stone continue to heat for 15–30 minutes longer, without opening the door.

On a floured pizza peel, stretch or roll out the pizza dough into a 12-inch (30-cm) round. If the dough springs back, let it rest for about 10 minutes before continuing. Leaving a 1-inch (2.5-cm) border, spread the pesto over the dough round. Dollop the ricotta all over the pizza. Distribute the tomato halves evenly around the pizza and sprinkle with the Parmesan. Brush the outside edge of the dough with olive oil and season the whole pizza lightly with salt and pepper.

Carefully slide the pizza from the peel onto the hot stone in the oven and bake for 10–12 minutes, or until the crust is golden brown. Using the peel, transfer the pizza to a cutting board. Let cool for a few minutes, then scatter the basil over the top, slice, and serve.

SERVES 4

4 tablespoons (2 fl oz/60 ml) olive oil, plus more for brushing

1 small red onion, halved lengthwise and thinly sliced crosswise

Kosher salt and freshly ground pepper

8 oz (250 g) white or brown mushrooms, brushed clean and thickly sliced

5 oz (155 g) baby kale or stemmed (including tough center spines) and chopped regular kale

1 ball Deep-Dish Pizza Dough (page 18)

1 cup (8 fl oz/250 ml) Tomato Sauce (page 26)

1¼ cups (5 oz/155 g) shredded low-moisture mozzarella cheese

DEEP-DISH PIZZA WITH MUSHROOMS, RED ONION & KALE

Position a rack in the lower third of the oven and preheat to 400°F (200°C).

In a frying pan over medium-high heat, warm 1 tablespoon of the olive oil. Add the onion and season with salt and pepper. Sauté until the onion is soft and beginning to brown, about 7 minutes. Transfer to a large plate; don't wipe out the pan.

Add another 2 tablespoons of the olive oil to the pan, warm briefly, and add the mushrooms. Season with salt and pepper and cook, stirring a few times, until the mushrooms soften and begin to brown, about 5 minutes. Transfer to the plate with the onion. Again, don't wipe out the pan.

Add the remaining 1 tablespoon olive oil and the kale to the pan. Season the kale with salt and pepper and sauté until it wilts, about 4 minutes. Transfer to the plate with the onion and mushroom slices.

Brush a 10-inch (25-cm) cast-iron frying pan with olive oil. Put the pizza dough in the pan and pat into a disk. Using your hands, press the dough into the pan, nudging it gently into an even layer on the bottom and about halfway up the sides. Brush the dough with more olive oil and top with the onions, mushrooms, and kale. Pour the tomato sauce over, spread it evenly, and finish with the cheese. Season the whole pizza lightly with salt and pepper.

Transfer the pan to the oven and bake for 30–40 minutes, or until the bottom of the dough is nicely browned (lift with a spatula or long-bladed knife to peek). Remove from the oven, let cool for 5 minutes. Slice the pizza directly in the pan, and serve right away.

SERVES 4

ONE-POT SOLUTION

Deep-dish pizza is an easy one-pot dish. Use this recipe for a basic vegetarian dinner, substituting your favorite vegetables as you see fit.

3 tablespoons olive oil, plus more for brushing

8 oz (250 g) white or brown mushrooms, brushed clean and thickly sliced

Kosher salt and freshly ground pepper

1 ball Thin-Crust Pizza Dough (page 17) or Whole-Wheat Pizza Dough (page 20)

1 cup (8 fl oz/250 ml) Tomato Sauce (page 26)

2 cups (8 oz/250 g) shredded low-moisture mozzarella cheese

4 oz (125 g) salami, thinly sliced and cut into ½-inch (12-mm) strips

¾ cup (4 oz/125 g) pitted, brine-cured black olives, halved lengthwise

MUSHROOM, SALAMI & BLACK OLIVE PIZZA

Place a pizza stone in the middle of the oven and preheat to 450°F (230°C). Once the oven has reached 450°F (230°C), let the stone continue to heat for 15–30 minutes longer, without opening the door.

In a frying pan over medium-high heat, warm the olive oil. Add the mushrooms and season with salt and pepper. Sauté until softened and slightly browned around the edges, about 5 minutes. Remove from the heat and set aside.

On a floured pizza peel, stretch or roll out the pizza dough into a 12-inch (30-cm) round. If the dough springs back, let it rest for about 10 minutes before continuing. Leaving a 1-inch (2.5-cm) border, spread the sauce over the dough round and top with the cheese. Distribute the salami, mushrooms, and olives evenly around the pizza. Brush the outside edge of the dough with olive oil and lightly season the whole pizza with salt and pepper.

Carefully slide the pizza from the peel onto the hot stone in the oven and bake for 10–12 minutes, or until the crust is golden brown. Using the peel, transfer the pizza to a cutting board. Let cool for a few minutes, then slice and serve right away.

SERVES 4

BRING THE PIZZERIA HOME

This classic pizza-parlor favorite is easy to assemble and always a crowd-pleaser. You can use any type of mushroom on this pizza; sautéing them first adds a sweet, caramelized flavor and gives them nice golden edges. Serve with a Chopped Salad (page 107) for a complete meal.

½ small red onion, thinly sliced

¾ teaspoon balsamic vinegar

Olive oil

Kosher salt and freshly ground pepper

FOR THE MINI MEATBALLS:

¼ lb (125 g) *each* ground pork and beef

1 clove garlic, minced

2 tablespoons grated Parmesan cheese

1 ball Thin-Crust Pizza Dough (page 17) or Whole-Wheat Pizza Dough (page 20)

1 cup (8 fl oz/250 ml) Tomato Sauce (page 26)

1¼ cups (5 oz/155 g) shredded low-moisture mozzarella cheese

¼ cup (1 oz/30 g) grated Parmesan cheese

MINI MEATBALL & RED ONION PIZZA

Make a double batch of these delicious meatballs; they freeze well and are a great way to add bursts of rich flavor to any pizza. To test the meatballs for seasoning before you roll the whole batch, make a small patty and fry it, then taste and adjust as needed.

Place a pizza stone in the middle of the oven and preheat to 450°F (230°C). Once the oven has reached 450°F (230°C), let the stone continue to heat for 15–30 minutes longer, without opening the door.

In a small bowl, toss the onion with the vinegar, ½ teaspoon olive oil, and salt and pepper to taste. Set aside.

To make the meatballs, in a large bowl, combine the pork and beef, the garlic, and the 2 tablespoons Parmesan. Season well with salt and pepper and mix gently with your hands. Form into mini meatballs, using a scant 1 teaspoon of the meat mixture for each and placing the finished meatballs on a plate as you work. Set aside.

On a floured pizza peel, stretch or roll out the pizza dough into a 12-inch (30-cm) oval, with even thickness across the oval. If the dough springs back, let it rest for about 10 minutes before continuing. Leaving a 1-inch (2.5-cm) border, spread the sauce over the dough and top with the mozzarella and the ¼ cup (1 oz/30 g) Parmesan. Distribute the meatballs evenly around the pizza and finish with the marinated onions. Brush the outside edge of the dough with olive oil and season the whole pizza lightly with salt and pepper.

Carefully slide the pizza from the peel onto the hot stone in the oven and bake for 10–12 minutes, or until the meatballs are cooked through and the crust is golden brown. Using the peel, transfer the pizza to a cutting board and scatter basil all over the top. Let cool for a few minutes, then slice and serve right away.

SERVES 4

1 ball Thin-Crust Pizza Dough (page 17) or Whole-Wheat Pizza Dough (page 20)

3 tablespoons olive oil

Kosher salt and freshly ground pepper

4 ripe plum tomatoes, thinly sliced

8 oz (250 g) small mozzarella balls (bocconcini), halved

¼ cup (1 oz/30 g) grated Parmesan cheese

4 oz (125 g) prosciutto, sliced paper-thin, torn into 2-inch (5-cm) pieces

Juice of ½ lemon

4 cups (4 oz/125 g) baby arugula

BOCCONCINI & PROSCIUTTO PIZZA WITH ARUGULA

Place a pizza stone in the middle of the oven and preheat to 450°F (230°C). Once the oven has reached 450°F (230°C), let the stone continue to heat for 15–30 minutes longer, without opening the door.

On a floured pizza peel, stretch or roll out the pizza dough into a 12-inch (30-cm) round. If the dough springs back, let it rest for about 10 minutes before continuing. Brush the entire dough round with 1 tablespoon of the olive oil and season lightly with salt and pepper. Leaving a 1-inch (2.5-cm) border, distribute the tomato slices and bocconcini halves evenly around the pizza. Top with the Parmesan and prosciutto.

Carefully slide the pizza from the peel onto the hot stone in the oven and bake for 10–12 minutes, or until the crust is golden brown.

Meanwhile, in the bottom of a large bowl, whisk together the remaining 2 tablespoons olive oil and the lemon juice. Season to taste with salt and pepper. Add the arugula and toss to coat.

Using the peel, transfer the pizza to a cutting board. Let cool for a few minutes, then top the pizza with the dressed arugula. Slice and serve right away.

SERVES 4

GIVE 'EM SOME GREENS

Topping pizza with a handful of lightly dressed greens is a great way to add more vegetables to dinner. Here, the slightly peppery taste of the arugula complements the saltiness of the cheese and prosciutto.

2 tablespoons olive oil, plus more for brushing

2 yellow onions, cut in half through the stem end and thinly sliced crosswise

Kosher salt and freshly ground pepper

1 tablespoon balsamic vinegar

5 oz (155 g) pancetta, cut into small cubes

1 ball Thin-Crust Pizza Dough (page 17) or Whole-Wheat Pizza Dough (page 20)

1 cup (8 fl oz/250 ml) Tomato Sauce (page 26)

1½ cups (6 oz/185 g) shredded low-moisture mozzarella cheese

6–8 fresh basil leaves, torn into large pieces

PANCETTA & CARAMELIZED ONION PIZZA

These simple toppings also taste delicious on a Cauliflower Crust (page 23). To save time, the onions can be made a day in advance or cut into half-moon shapes and roasted in a 400°F (200°C) oven for 30 minutes for hands-off cooking.

Warm the olive oil in a frying pan over high heat. Add the onions and sauté until translucent, about 8 minutes. Reduce the heat to medium-low and season well with salt and pepper. Cook slowly, stirring occasionally, until the onions turn a very deep brown, 35–45 minutes. Add the vinegar and stir until completely absorbed, about 2 minutes. Remove from the heat and set aside.

Place a pizza stone in the middle of the oven and preheat to 450°F (230°C). Once the oven has reached 450°F (230°C), let the stone continue to heat for 15–30 minutes longer, without opening the door.

In a clean frying pan over medium-high heat, fry the pancetta, stirring often, until cooked through and nicely browned, about 8 minutes. Using a slotted spoon, transfer to paper towels to drain.

On a floured pizza peel, stretch or roll out the pizza dough into a 12-inch (30-cm) round. If the dough springs back, let it rest for about 10 minutes before continuing. Leaving a 1-inch (2.5-cm) border, spread the sauce over the dough round and top with the cheese. Distribute the caramelized onions evenly around the pizza and top with the pancetta. Brush the outside edge of the dough with olive oil and season the whole pizza lightly with salt and pepper.

Carefully slide the pizza from the peel onto the hot stone in the oven and bake for 10–12 minutes, or until the crust is golden brown. Using the peel, transfer the pizza to a cutting board. Let cool for a few minutes, then scatter the basil over the top, slice, and serve.

SERVES 4

1 tablespoon olive oil, plus more for brushing

2 cloves garlic, minced

¾ lb (375 g) ground beef

2 green onions, white and tender
green parts only, sliced

Kosher salt and freshly ground pepper

1 ball Thin-Crust Pizza Dough (page 17) or
Whole-Wheat Pizza Dough (page 20)

1 cup (8 fl oz/250 ml) Tomato Sauce (page 26)

¾ cup (3 oz/90 g) shredded low-moisture
mozzarella cheese

¾ cup (3 oz/90 g) shredded Asiago cheese

½ cup (2½ oz/75 g) green olives,
pitted and sliced

GROUND BEEF, GREEN OLIVE & ASIAGO PIZZA

Place a pizza stone in the middle of the oven and preheat to 450°F (230°C). Once the oven has reached 450°F (230°C), let the stone continue to heat for 15–30 minutes longer, without opening the door.

Warm the olive oil in a frying pan over medium-high heat. Add the garlic and sauté just until it begins to soften but not brown, about 1 minute. Add the ground beef and cook, stirring occasionally and using your spoon to break up any clumps, until the meat is mostly browned (it will finish cooking in the oven). Using a slotted spoon, transfer the beef to a bowl. Add the green onions, season well with salt and pepper, and set aside.

On a floured pizza peel, stretch or roll out the pizza dough into a 12-inch (30-cm) round. If the dough springs back, let it rest for about 10 minutes before continuing. Leaving a 1-inch (2.5-cm) border, spread the sauce over the dough round and top with even layers of the mozzarella and Asiago. Distribute the ground beef and the olives evenly around the pizza. Brush the outside edge of the dough with olive oil and season the whole pizza lightly with salt and pepper.

Carefully slide the pizza from the peel onto the hot stone in the oven and bake for 10–12 minutes, or until the crust is golden brown. Using the peel, transfer the pizza to a cutting board. Let cool for a few minutes, then slice and serve right away.

SERVES 4

Asiago adds a sharp and salty touch to this creative pizza, but you could substitute half of the cheese with pepper Jack cheese for a spicy variation. For a complete meal, serve with broccolini sautéed in olive oil with a generous squeeze of fresh lemon juice.

1 ball Thin-Crust Pizza Dough (page 17) or
Whole-Wheat Pizza Dough (page 20)

4 tablespoons (2½ oz/75 g) fig jam

8 oz (250 g) Gorgonzola cheese, crumbled

3 oz (90 g) thinly sliced prosciutto

Olive oil for brushing

Kosher salt and freshly ground pepper

4 tablespoons (2 fl oz/60 ml) balsamic vinegar

FIG JAM, GORGONZOLA & PROSCIUTTO PIZZA

This decadent and richly-flavored pizza is finished off with a syrupy balsamic reduction. Make extra of this delicious condiment to drizzle over salads, roasted vegetables, and roasted meats.

Place a pizza stone in the middle of the oven and preheat to 450°F (230°C). Once the oven has reached 450°F (230°C), let the stone continue to heat for 15–30 minutes longer, without opening the door.

On a floured pizza peel, stretch or roll out the pizza dough into a 12-inch (30-cm) round. If the dough springs back, let it rest for about 10 minutes before continuing. Leaving a 1-inch (2.5-cm) border, spread the fig jam over the dough round and top with the cheese. Cover the pizza with the prosciutto. Brush the outside edge of the dough with olive oil and season the whole pizza lightly with salt and pepper.

Carefully slide the pizza from the peel onto the hot stone in the oven and bake for 10–12 minutes, or until the crust is golden brown.

To make the balsamic syrup, pour the vinegar into a small, heavy-bottomed saucepan and place over high heat. Bring to a gentle boil, then reduce the heat to low and let the vinegar simmer gently until very thick, 6–8 minutes. Remove from the heat and let cool slightly. (If you let the syrup sit too long, it will harden. Simply return to a low heat to soften.)

Using the peel, transfer the pizza to a cutting board. Drizzle the balsamic reduction all over the top of the pizza. Let cool for a few minutes, then slice and serve right away.

SERVES 4

2 small red bell peppers

1 ball Thin-Crust Pizza Dough (page 17) or Whole-Wheat Pizza Dough (page 20)

1 cup (8 fl oz/250 ml) Tomato Sauce (page 26)

2 cups (8 oz/250 g) shredded low-moisture mozzarella cheese

¼ cup (1 oz/30 g) grated Parmesan cheese

3 oz (90 g) pepperoni, thinly sliced

Olive oil for brushing

Kosher salt and freshly ground pepper

8 fresh basil leaves, torn into large pieces

PEPPERONI, ROASTED RED PEPPER & MOZZARELLA PIZZA

Place a pizza stone in the middle of the oven and preheat to 450°F (230°C). Once the oven has reached 450°F (230°C), let the stone continue to heat for 15–30 minutes longer, without opening the door.

Using tongs or a large fork, hold 1 pepper at a time directly over the flame of a gas burner, or place directly on the grate. Roast, turning as needed, until blistered and charred black on all sides, 10–15 minutes total. (Alternatively, place the peppers under a preheated broiler, as close as possible to the heating element, and roast to char them on all sides, turning as needed.) Transfer the peppers to a bowl, cover with plastic wrap or a clean kitchen towel, and set aside to steam until cooled, about 20 minutes. Once cool, peel or rub away the charred skins, then seed and chop the peppers. Set aside.

On a floured pizza peel, stretch or roll out the pizza dough into a 12-inch (30-cm) oval, with even thickness across the oval. If the dough springs back, let it rest for about 10 minutes before continuing. Leaving a 1-inch (2.5-cm) border, spread the sauce over the dough round and top with the cheeses. Distribute the roasted peppers and the pepperoni evenly around the pizza. Brush the outside edge of the dough with olive oil and season the whole pizza lightly with salt and pepper.

Carefully slide the pizza from the peel onto the hot stone in the oven and bake for 10–12 minutes, or until the crust is golden brown. Using the peel, transfer the pizza to a cutting board. Let cool for a few minutes, then scatter the basil over the top, slice, and serve.

SERVES 4

FRESH TWIST ON A CLASSIC

Here, classic pepperoni pizza gets a lift from chunks of red bell pepper and basil leaves. For an equally tasty variation, replace the pepperoni with torn pieces of sliced prosciutto.

1 tablespoon olive oil, plus more for brushing

2 cloves garlic, minced

8 oz (250 g) baby spinach leaves

Kosher salt and freshly ground pepper

1 ball Thin-Crust Pizza Dough (page 17) or Whole-Wheat Pizza Dough (page 20)

1 cup (8 fl oz/250 ml) Tomato Sauce (page 26)

1½ cups (6 oz/185 g) shredded low-moisture mozzarella cheese

⅓ lb (155 g) fresh chorizo, ground or removed from casings

CHORIZO & SAUTÉED GREENS PIZZA

SUBSTITUTION SOLUTIONS

————— >>>>>>>>>

Fresh chorizo is a Mexican sausage that has a serious kick; use sweet Italian sausage for a milder flavor. In this recipe, the spinach is sautéed with olive oil and garlic to give it extra flavor. You can substitute any hearty greens that you like, such as kale, chard, or collard greens.

Place a pizza stone in the middle of the oven and preheat to 450°F (230°C). Once the oven has reached 450°F (230°C), let the stone continue to heat for 15–30 minutes longer, without opening the door.

Warm the olive oil in a frying pan over medium heat. Add the garlic and sauté until soft but not browned, about 2 minutes. Add the spinach, season with salt and pepper, and cook, stirring often, until the spinach mostly wilts, about 2 minutes. Remove from the heat and set aside.

On a floured pizza peel, stretch or roll out the pizza dough into a 12-inch (30-cm) round. If the dough springs back, let it rest for about 10 minutes before continuing. Leaving a 1-inch (2.5-cm) border, spread the sauce over the dough round and top with the cheese. Distribute the sautéed spinach and the chorizo evenly around the pizza, breaking up the sausage with your fingers as needed. Brush the outside edge of the dough with olive oil and season the whole pizza lightly with salt and pepper.

Carefully slide the pizza from the peel onto the hot stone in the oven and bake for 10–12 minutes, or until the chorizo is cooked through and the crust is golden brown. Let cool for a few minutes, then slice and serve right away.

SERVES 4

¾ lb (375 g) sweet or hot Italian sausage, casings removed

1 small red bell pepper, seeded and chopped

5 oz (155 g) white or brown mushrooms, brushed clean and sliced

Kosher salt and freshly ground pepper

Olive oil for brushing

1 ball Deep-Dish Pizza Dough (page 18)

1½ oz (45 g) pepperoni, sliced

⅓ cup (2 oz/60 g) oil-cured black olives, pitted and halved

1 cup (8 fl oz/250 ml) Tomato Sauce (page 26)

1¼ cups (5 oz/155 g) shredded low-moisture mozzarella cheese

FULLY-LOADED DEEP-DISH PIZZA

Position a rack in the lower third of the oven and preheat to 400°F (200°C).

In a frying pan over medium-high heat, fry the sausage, stirring occasionally and using your spoon to break up any clumps, until cooked through, about 8 minutes. Using a slotted spoon, transfer to paper towels to drain.

Pour off all but 1 tablespoon of the fat in the pan and return to medium-high heat. Add the bell pepper and mushrooms to the pan, season with salt and pepper, and sauté until the vegetables are softened and the mushrooms are browned around the edges, about 5 minutes. Remove from the heat and set aside.

Brush a 10-inch (25-cm) cast-iron frying pan with olive oil. Put the pizza dough in the pan and pat into a disk. Using your hands, press the dough into the pan, nudging it gently into an even layer on the bottom and about halfway up the sides. Brush the dough with more olive oil and top with the sausage, pepper and mushroom mixture, pepperoni, and olives. Pour the tomato sauce over, spread it evenly, and finish with the cheese. Season the whole pizza lightly with salt and pepper.

Transfer the pan to the oven and bake until the bottom of the dough is nicely browned (lift carefully with a spatula or long-bladed knife to peek). Remove from the oven and let cool for 5 minutes. Slice directly in the pan and serve right away.

SERVES 4

DINNER, CHICAGO-STYLE

Hearty deep-dish pies offer a great opportunity to load up on ingredients and different flavors. You don't need a special plan to make delicious deep-dish pizza—a cast-iron frying pan does the trick.

1 ball Thin-Crust Pizza Dough (page 17) or Whole-Wheat Pizza Dough (page 20)

1 cup (4 oz/125 g) shredded low-moisture mozzarella cheese

3 ripe plum tomatoes, thinly sliced

½ lb (250 g) fennel sausage, removed from casings

½ cup (4 oz/125 g) whole-milk ricotta cheese

Olive oil for brushing

Kosher salt and freshly ground pepper

Fresh rosemary or basil leaves for garnish

FENNEL SAUSAGE, RICOTTA & FRESH TOMATO PIZZA

FRESH & FLAVORFUL

Aromatic fennel seed gives sausage a wonderful taste. If you can't find it, substitute sweet or spicy Italian sausage, chorizo, or linguiça. Using fresh tomato slices in lieu of sauce not only shortens our prep time, but adds extra freshness to each bite.

Place a pizza stone in the middle of the oven and preheat to 450°F (230°C). Once the oven has reached 450°F (230°C), let the stone continue to heat for 15–30 minutes longer, without opening the door.

On a floured pizza peel, stretch or roll out the pizza dough into a 12-inch (30-cm) round. If the dough springs back, let it rest for about 10 minutes before continuing. Leaving a 1-inch (2.5-cm) border, cover the dough round with the mozzarella and arrange the tomato slices on top. Distribute the sausage evenly around the pizza, breaking it up with your fingers as needed. Dollop the ricotta all over the pizza. Brush the outside edge of the dough with olive oil and season the whole pizza lightly with salt and pepper.

Carefully slide the pizza from the peel onto the hot stone in the oven and bake for 10–12 minutes, or until the sausage is cooked through and the crust is golden brown. Using the peel, transfer the pizza to a cutting board and scatter the rosemary over the top. Let cool for a few minutes, then slice and serve right away.

SERVES 4

2 tablespoons unsalted butter

2 teaspoons sugar

½ fresh pineapple, peeled and cut into 4 slices about ½ inch (12 mm) thick

1 ball Thin-Crust Pizza Dough (page 17) or Whole-Wheat Pizza Dough (page 20)

1 cup (8 fl oz/250 ml) Tomato Sauce (page 26)

1½ cups (6 oz/185 g) shredded low-moisture mozzarella cheese

3 oz (90 g) soppresatta, thinly sliced and cut into ½-inch (12-mm) strips

Olive oil for brushing

Kosher salt and freshly ground pepper

CARAMELIZED PINEAPPLE & SOPPRESATTA PIZZA

ALOHA PIE

>>>>>>>>>>

This riff on a Hawaiian-style pie is a kid-friendly treat. Reduce the amount of sugar for the pineapple if the fruit is very ripe. Make some extra caramelized pineapple for a simple dessert served on top of vanilla ice cream.

Place a pizza stone in the middle of the oven and preheat to 450°F (230°C). Once the oven has reached 450°F (230°C), let the stone continue to heat for 15–30 minutes longer, without opening the door.

In a large frying pan over medium-high heat, melt the butter. Sprinkle the sugar over the butter and allow the butter to brown slightly. Add the pineapple slices and cook, turning once, until they caramelize, about 5 minutes per side. Transfer to a plate and let cool, then cut into ½-inch (12-mm) dice. If the center core is too hard, discard.

On a floured pizza peel, stretch or roll out the pizza dough into a 12-inch (30-cm) round. If the dough springs back, let it rest for about 10 minutes before continuing. Leaving a 1-inch (2.5-cm) border, spread the sauce over the dough round and top with the cheese. Distribute the pineapple and the soppresatta evenly around the pizza. Brush the outside edge of the dough with olive oil and season the whole pizza lightly with salt and pepper.

Carefully slide the pizza from the peel onto the hot stone in the oven and bake for 10–12 minutes, or until the crust is golden brown. Using the peel, transfer the pizza to a cutting board. Let cool for a few minutes, then slice and serve right away.

SERVES 4

1 bone-in, skin-on chicken breast, about ¾ lb (375 g)

3 tablespoons olive oil, plus more for brushing

Kosher salt and freshly ground pepper

2 cloves garlic, minced

5 oz (155 g) baby kale or stemmed (including tough center spines) and chopped regular kale

1 ball Thin-Crust Pizza Dough (page 17) or Whole-Wheat Pizza Dough (page 20)

1 cup (8 fl oz/250 ml) White Pizza Sauce (page 30)

2 cups (8 oz/250 g) shredded smoked Cheddar cheese

KALE, CHICKEN & SMOKED CHEDDAR PIZZA

Preheat the oven to 375°F (190°C). Pat the chicken dry and put it on a small baking sheet. Brush with 1 tablespoon of the olive oil and season well with salt and pepper. Bake the chicken until opaque throughout, about 25 minutes. Remove from the oven, and when cool enough to handle, discard the skin and bone and shred the chicken into bite-sized pieces. Set aside.

Raise the oven temperature to 450°F (230°C) and place a pizza stone on the middle rack. Once the oven has reached 450°F (230°C), let the stone continue to heat for 15–30 minutes longer, without opening the door.

In a frying pan over medium-high heat, warm the remaining 2 tablespoons oil. Add the garlic and sauté until softened, about 1 minute. Add the kale, season with salt and pepper, and sauté until wilted, about 3 minutes. Remove from the heat and set aside.

On a floured pizza peel, stretch or roll out the dough into a 12-inch (30-cm) round. If the dough springs back, let it rest for about 10 minutes before continuing. Leaving a 1-inch (2.5-cm) border, spread the white sauce over the dough round and top with the cheese. Distribute the chicken and the kale evenly around the pizza. Brush the outside edge of the dough with olive oil and season the whole pizza lightly with salt and pepper.

Carefully slide the pizza from the peel onto the hot stone in the oven and bake for 10–12 minutes, or until the crust is golden brown. Using the peel, transfer the pizza to a cutting board. Brush the tops of the chicken pieces with a little more olive oil. Let cool for a few minutes, then slice and serve right away.

SERVES 4

WHOLESOME PIE

With protein from the chicken, calcium from the cheese along with nutrient-packed kale, this pizza is a complete meal. The recipe calls for roasting a chicken breast, but it's also a great way to use up the last bit of meat from a rotisserie chicken. Just pull the meat from the precooked bird into bite-size pieces and toss with the olive oil, salt, and pepper.

1 boneless, skinless chicken breast, about ½ lb (250 g)

6 teaspoons olive oil, plus more for brushing and drizzling

1 teaspoon Chinese five-spice powder

Kosher salt and freshly ground pepper

1 Chinese eggplant, cut on the diagonal into ¼-inch (6-mm) slices

1 small red onion, thinly sliced

1 ball Thin-Crust Pizza Dough (page 17) or Whole-Wheat Pizza Dough (page 20)

1½ cups (6 oz/185 g) grated Parmesan cheese

6–8 fresh Thai or regular basil leaves, torn into large pieces

FIVE-SPICE CHICKEN, CHINESE EGGPLANT & THAI BASIL PIZZA

Preheat the oven to 400°F (200°C). Pat the chicken dry and put it on a small baking sheet. Brush with 2 teaspoons of the olive oil, and season on both sides with the five-spice powder and salt and pepper. Bake until opaque throughout, 20–25 minutes. Remove from the oven, and when cool enough to handle, transfer to a bowl, and shred the chicken into bite-sized pieces. Combine with any left behind oil and spices.

Prepare the eggplant according to directions at right.

Raise the oven temperature to 450°F (230°C) and place a pizza stone on the middle rack. Once the oven has reached 450°F (230°C), let the stone continue to heat for 15–30 minutes longer, without opening the door.

In a small bowl, toss the red onion with the remaining 1 teaspoon oil and season with salt and pepper. Set aside. On a floured pizza peel, stretch or roll out the pizza dough into a 12-inch (30-cm) round. If the dough springs back, let it rest for about 10 minutes before continuing. Brush the entire dough round with olive oil and season with salt and pepper. Leaving a 1-inch (2.5-cm) border, cover the dough with the cheese. Distribute the eggplant, shredded chicken, and marinated onion evenly around the pizza.

Carefully slide the pizza from the peel onto the hot stone in the oven and bake for 10–12 minutes, or until the crust is golden brown. Using the peel, transfer the pizza to a cutting board. Let cool for a few minutes, then scatter the basil over the top, slice, and serve.

SERVES 4

To make baked eggplant slices, preheat the oven to 400°F (200°C). Arrange the eggplant slices in a single layer on a baking sheet. Brush all sides with 3 teaspoons oil and season with salt and pepper. Roast for 10 minutes, then, using tongs, flip the slices. Return to roast until the slices are fork-tender and browned around the edges, about 5 minutes. Remove from the oven and set aside.

6 slices thick-cut bacon

¾ cup (2 oz/60 g) Brussels sprouts, halved and cored, outer leaves kept whole and the rest sliced

1 small red onion, thinly sliced

Kosher salt and freshly ground pepper

1½ teaspoons balsamic vinegar

1 ball Thin-Crust Pizza Dough (page 17) or Whole-Wheat Pizza Dough (page 20)

1 cup (8 fl oz/250 ml) Tomato Sauce (page 26)

8 oz (250 g) fresh mozzarella cheese, preferably buffalo, diced

BRUSSELS SPROUTS & BACON PIZZA

EVERYTHING'S BETTER WITH BACON

→ >>>>>>>>

Serving shaved Brussels sprouts on a pizza is a great way to introduce younger kids to this strong-tasting vegetable. Here, they are cooked with red onion and finished with a touch of balsamic vinegar to sweeten them up.

Place a pizza stone in the middle of the oven and preheat to 450°F (230°C). Once the oven has reached 450°F (230°C), let the stone continue to heat for an additional 15–30 minutes, without opening the door.

In a frying pan over medium-high heat, fry the bacon until crisp, about 6 minutes. Transfer to paper towels to drain. When the bacon is cool enough to handle, crumble or tear it into bite-sized pieces. Set aside.

Pour off all but 1 tablespoon of the fat in the pan and return to medium-high heat. Add the Brussels sprouts and onion to the pan, season with salt and pepper, and sauté until the vegetables soften and begin to brown, about 5 minutes. Stir in the vinegar and sauté until the liquid is absorbed, about 2 minutes. Remove from the heat and set aside.

On a floured pizza peel, stretch or roll out the pizza dough into a rectangle or a 12-inch (30-cm) square, with even thickness across the square. If the dough springs back, let it rest for about 10 minutes before continuing. Leaving a 1-inch (2.5-cm) border, spread the sauce over the dough and top with the cheese. Distribute the Brussels sprouts and bacon evenly around the pizza. Brush the outside edge of the dough with olive oil and season the whole pizza lightly with salt and pepper.

Carefully slide the pizza from the peel onto the hot stone in the oven and bake for 10–12 minutes, or until the crust is golden brown. Using the peel, transfer the pizza to a cutting board. Let cool for a few minutes, then slice and serve right away.

SERVES 4

3 tablespoons olive oil, plus more for brushing

5 cloves garlic, thinly sliced

¾ teaspoon red pepper flakes

1 cup (8 fl oz/250 ml) Tomato Sauce (page 26) or White Pizza Sauce (page 30)

1 ball Thin-Crust Pizza Dough (page 17) or Whole-Wheat Pizza Dough (page 20)

1½ cups (6 oz/185 g) shredded low-moisture mozzarella cheese

1 cup (5 oz/155 g) kalamata olives, pitted and halved lengthwise

¼ cup (2 oz/60 g) brined capers, drained

8 anchovy fillets

5 fresh basil leaves, torn (optional)

SPICY KALAMATA OLIVE, ANCHOVY & CAPER PIZZA

LUSTY & GUTSY

>>>>>>>>>

All the ingredients of a classic puttanesca sauce come together in this rich and delicious pizza. Be careful when seasoning this pizza, as many of the toppings are naturally salty. Serve with a Caprese Salad (page 111).

Place a pizza stone in the middle of the oven and preheat to 450°F (230°C). Once the oven has reached 450°F (230°C), let the stone continue to heat for 15–30 minutes longer, without opening the door.

Warm the olive oil in a small frying pan over low heat. Add the garlic and red pepper flakes and sauté just until the garlic begins to soften but not brown, about 1 minute. Transfer to a bowl. Pour in the tomato or white sauce and stir to mix well. Set aside.

On a floured pizza peel, stretch or roll out the pizza dough into a 12-inch (30-cm) oval, with even thickness across the oval. If the dough springs back, let it rest for about 10 minutes before continuing. Leaving a 1-inch (2.5-cm) border, spread the sauce over the dough and top with the cheese. Distribute the olives, capers, and anchovies evenly around the pizza. Brush the outside edge of the dough with olive oil.

Carefully slide the pizza from the peel onto the hot stone in the oven and bake for 10–12 minutes, or until the crust is golden brown. Using the peel, transfer the pizza to a cutting board. Let cool for a few minutes, then scatter the basil over the top, if using, slice, and serve.

SERVES 4

WHAT YOU NEED

1 cup (8 oz/250 g) crème fraîche or sour cream

1 tablespoon fresh lemon juice

Grated zest of 1 lemon

2 tablespoons chopped fresh dill, plus small sprigs for garnish

2 tablespoons chopped fresh chives

Kosher salt and freshly ground pepper

½ small red onion, thinly sliced

1 tablespoon olive oil, plus more for brushing

1 ball Thin-Crust Pizza Dough (page 17)

8 oz (250 g) thinly sliced smoked salmon, chopped or torn into small pieces

SMOKED SALMON & RED ONION PIZZETTES

Place a pizza stone in the middle of the oven and preheat to 450°F (230°C). Once the oven has reached 450°F (230°C), let the stone heat for 15–30 minutes longer, without opening the door.

In a small bowl, stir together the crème fraîche, lemon juice and zest, dill, and chives. Season with salt and pepper to taste. Set aside at room temperature.

In a small bowl, toss the onion with the olive oil and season lightly with salt and pepper. Set aside.

Divide the pizza dough into 8 equal pieces. On a floured pizza peel, roll out each piece into a 5-inch (13-cm) round. Brush each dough round with olive oil and season lightly with salt and pepper. Top with the onion slices, dividing them evenly.

Carefully slide the pizzettes from the peel onto the hot stone in the oven and bake until the crusts are lightly browned, about 6 minutes.

Using the peel, transfer the pizzettes to a board or serving platter. Let cool for a few minutes, then dollop 2 tablespoons of the crème fraîche on each. Scatter the smoked salmon on top of the pizzettes, dividing it evenly. Garnish each with a sprig of dill and serve right away.

SERVES 4–6

MAKE IT SPECIAL

Serve these elegant and versatile pizzettes for a light dinner in warm weather with a crisp white wine and the Haricots Verts & Cherry Tomato Salad (page 116). Baking the onions on the dough helps to mellow the flavor and sweeten the taste.

3 tablespoons olive oil, plus more
for brushing and drizzling

5 shallots, thinly sliced

Kosher salt and freshly ground pepper

2 teaspoons balsamic vinegar

2 tablespoons fresh rosemary leaves, chopped

1 ball Thin-Crust Pizza Dough (page 17)

1 small apple, cored and thinly sliced

8 oz (250 g) Brie cheese, thickly sliced and
cut into 1-inch (2.5-cm) pieces

BRIE & APPLE PIZZETTES WITH ROSEMARY & SHALLOTS

MINI PIES

These little pizzas are a great
choice for a fall dinner (or as
an appetizer for a dinner party).
The caramelized shallots add
deep flavor and complement
the apples and cheese.

Place a pizza stone in the middle of the oven and preheat to 450°F (230°C). Once the oven has reached 450°F (230°C), let the stone continue to heat for 15–30 minutes longer, without opening the door.

In a small frying pan, warm the olive oil over medium-high heat. Add the shallots and sauté until translucent, about 4 minutes. Reduce the heat to low, season with salt and pepper, and cook, stirring occasionally, until the shallots caramelize and turn deep brown, about 20 minutes longer. Stir in the vinegar and rosemary and cook for another 2 minutes. Remove from the heat and set aside.

Divide the pizza dough into 8 equal pieces. On a floured pizza peel, roll out each piece into a 5-inch (13-cm) round. Brush each dough round with olive oil and season lightly with salt and pepper.

Carefully slide the pizzettes from the peel onto the hot stone in the oven and bake until the crusts are starting to brown, about 7 minutes. Using the peel, remove the pizzettes from the oven and top with the apple slices and Brie, dividing them evenly. Top each with the caramelized shallot mixture.

Return the pizzettes to the oven and bake just until the cheese melts slightly and the crusts are golden brown, 3–4 minutes longer. Transfer to a serving platter and drizzle each with a little more olive oil. Let cool for a few minutes, then serve.

SERVES 4–6

---

1 small globe eggplant, diced

3 tablespoons olive oil

Kosher salt and freshly ground pepper

1 ball Thin-Crust Pizza Dough (page 17)

8 tablespoons Roasted Red Pepper Pesto (page 31) or Tomato Sauce (page 26)

8 basil leaves

8 tablespoons (2 oz/60 g) shredded low-moisture mozzarella cheese

2 tablespoons grated Parmesan cheese

1 large egg, beaten

EGGPLANT, MOZZARELLA & BASIL CALZONES

Preheat the oven to 400°F (200°C).

Pile the eggplant on a baking sheet lined with parchment paper. Drizzle with the olive oil, season well with salt and pepper, and toss to coat. Spread out the eggplant in a single layer and roast in the middle of the oven, stirring once about halfway through, until fork-tender, about 25 minutes. Remove from the oven and set aside.

Place a pizza stone in the oven and raise the oven temperature to 450°F (230°C). Once the oven has reached 450°F (230°C), let the stone continue to heat for 15–30 minutes longer, without opening the door.

Divide the pizza dough into 4 equal pieces. On a floured pizza peel, roll out each piece into a 6-inch (15-cm) round. Leaving a ½-inch (12-mm) border, top one half of each dough round with 2 tablespoons of the sauce; about ¼ cup (1½ oz/45 g) of the roasted eggplant; 2 basil leaves, torn into large pieces; 2 tablespoons of the mozzarella; and ½ tablespoon of the Parmesan. Season lightly with salt and pepper.

Fold the uncovered half of each calzone up and over the filling to meet the opposite edges, and crimp the edges of the dough tightly to seal. Using a pastry brush, brush the tops of the calzones with the egg. Using the tip of a sharp knife, make a slit in the top of each calzone.

Carefully slide the calzones from the peel onto the hot stone in the oven and bake until the crusts are golden brown, 8–10 minutes. Using the peel, transfer the calzones to a cutting board or wire rack and let cool for 5 minutes, then serve right away.

SERVES 4

MAKE MORE TO STORE

Calzones are delicious right out the oven, but they also freeze well. For a quick kid-friendly dinner, make smaller calzones to freeze for a midweek meal. To thaw, microwave until heated all the way through, 3–4 minutes. These calzones are also good made with basil pesto or even tapenade.

½ lb (500 g) sweet Italian sausages, removed from casings

1 ball Thin-Crust Pizza Dough (page 17) or Whole-Wheat Pizza Dough (page 20)

½ cup (4 fl oz/125 ml) Tomato Sauce (page 26)

1 cup (4 oz/125 g) shredded low-moisture mozzarella cheese

2 tablespoons grated Parmesan cheese

4 tablespoons pickled peperoncini, or to taste, drained and sliced

4–6 fresh basil leaves, torn into large pieces

Kosher salt and freshly ground pepper

1 large egg, beaten

SAUSAGE, PEPERONCINI & MOZZARELLA CALZONE

Making one big calzone takes a little bit less time than creating individual calzones, but you can easily divide the dough and make 4 or even 8 smaller ones. The peperoncini give this calzone a spicy kick.

Place a pizza stone in the middle of the oven and preheat to 450°F (230°C). Once the oven has reached 450°F (230°C), let the stone continue to heat for 15–30 minutes longer, without opening the door.

In a frying pan over medium-high heat, cook the sausages, using your spoon to break up any clumps, until the meat is cooked all the way through, about 6 minutes. Using a slotted spoon, transfer to paper towels to drain.

On a floured pizza peel, roll out the pizza dough into a 12-inch (30-cm) round. If the dough springs back, let it rest for about 10 minutes before continuing. Leaving a 1-inch (2.5-cm) border, spread half of the tomato sauce over one half of the dough round. Top with the sausage, mozzarella, Parmesan, peperoncini, and torn basil , then top with the remaining sauce. Season lightly with salt and pepper.

Fold the uncovered side of the dough up and over the filling to meet the opposite edges, and crimp the edges tightly to seal. Using a pastry brush, brush the top of the calzone with the egg. Make 2 slits in the top of the dough with the tip of a sharp knife.

Carefully slide the calzone from the peel onto the hot stone in the oven and bake until the crust is golden brown, 15–18 minutes. Using the peel, transfer the calzone to a cutting board and let rest for 5 minutes. Carefully slice and serve right away.

SERVES 2–4

1 ball Thin-Crust Pizza Dough (page 17) or Whole-Wheat Pizza Dough (page 20)

½ cup (4 fl oz/125 ml) Basil Pesto (page 29)

1 red bell pepper, roasted (see page 71)

1 cup (4 oz/125 g) shredded low-moisture mozzarella cheese

½ cup (4 oz/125 g) whole-milk ricotta cheese

¼ cup (1 oz/30 g) grated Parmesan cheese

Kosher salt and freshly ground pepper

1 large egg, beaten

THREE-CHEESE STROMBOLI WITH PESTO & RED PEPPERS

Place a pizza stone in the middle of the oven and preheat to 450°F (230°C). Once the oven has reached 450°F (230°C), let the stone heat for 15–30 minutes longer, without opening the oven door.

On a floured pizza peel, stretch or roll out the pizza dough into a 10-by-14-inch (25-by-35-cm) rectangle. If the dough springs back, let it rest for about 10 minutes before continuing. With a long side facing you, spread the pesto over the dough, leaving a 1-inch (2.5-cm) border on each short side and a 3-inch (7.5-cm) border on the long side farthest away from you. Scatter the roasted pepper over the pesto. In a bowl, stir together the cheeses, season with salt and pepper, and dollop all over the pesto and roasted peppers.

Using a pastry brush, brush the beaten egg on the uncovered edges of the dough. Fold over the 2 short sides to the 1-inch (2.5-cm) mark and brush the tops with the egg. Keeping the short sides tucked in, tightly roll up the stromboli lengthwise away from you. Crimp the seams tightly to seal and turn the stromboli seam side down on the peel. Brush the stromboli all over with the egg. Using the tip of a sharp knife, make a few slits along the top of the dough, about 2 inches (5 cm) apart. Season the outside lightly with salt and pepper.

Carefully slide the stromboli from the peel onto the hot stone in the oven, keeping it seam side down. Bake until the crust is golden brown, 15–18 minutes. Using the peel, transfer the stromboli to a cutting board and let rest for 5 minutes. Carefully cut crosswise into slices and serve right away.

SERVES 2-4

PARTY NIGHT

Stromboli is a good choice for a casual party, since it's simple to make a few different varieties and offer your guests slices of each. This basic recipe can be used for a range of fillings. Try: pepperoni and olives; roasted zucchini and squash; or spinach, mushrooms, and feta.

3 peaches, about ¾ lb (375 g) total, pitted and cut into thin wedges

2 teaspoons olive oil, plus more for brushing and drizzling

2 teaspoons balsamic vinegar

Kosher salt and freshly ground pepper

1 ball Thin-Crust Pizza Dough (page 17)

12 oz (375 g) fresh mozzarella cheese, preferably buffalo, thinly sliced

3 oz (90 g) prosciutto, sliced paper-thin, torn into 2-inch (5-cm) pieces

Small handful baby arugula

GRILLED PIZZA WITH MOZZARELLA, PROSCIUTTO & PEACHES

Build a medium-hot fire in a charcoal grill or preheat a gas grill to medium-high. In a bowl, toss the peaches with the 2 teaspoons olive oil, the vinegar, and salt and pepper to taste. Arrange the peaches on the grill grate and cook until nicely grill-marked, about 3 minutes per side. Transfer to a plate.

On a floured work surface, stretch or roll out the pizza dough until it is about ¼ inch (6 mm) thick (about a 10-inch/25-cm round). If the dough springs back, let it rest for about 10 minutes before continuing. Brush the top with olive oil and season lightly with salt and pepper. Place the dough round on the grill, oiled side down. Cook until there are nice dark grill marks on the first side, about 6 minutes.

Transfer the pizza to a work surface, grilled side down. Brush the second side with olive oil and season with salt and pepper, then turn the pizza grilled side up. Distribute the cheese, prosciutto, grilled peaches, and basil, torn into pieces, evenly around the pizza, and season again with salt and pepper.

Carefully return the pizza to the grill, cover, and grill until the cheese is melted and the dough is cooked through, about 5 minutes. Transfer the pizza to a cutting board and drizzle with a little more olive oil. Let cool for a few minutes, then slice and serve right away.

SERVES 4

GRILL PARTY

Grilling pizza is a great way to entertain. Once the dough is made and the toppings are chopped, it only takes a few minutes to cook the pie. Your guests will love the browned, smoky crust. Cooking pizza on the grill is easier when you shape the dough into small rectangles or rounds, which are better sized for the spatula crucial for getting the pizza on and off the grill.

1 ball Thin-Crust Pizza Dough (page 17) or Whole-Wheat Pizza Dough (page 20)

¾ cup (6 fl oz/180 ml) Roasted Red Pepper Pesto (page 31)

1 cup (5 oz/155 g) crumbled feta cheese

2 tablespoons fresh oregano leaves

½ lb (250 g) medium shrimp, peeled, deveined, and halved lengthwise

1 tablespoon olive oil, plus more for brushing

Kosher salt and freshly ground pepper

SHRIMP & FETA PIZZA WITH ROASTED RED PEPPER PESTO

ON A BUDGET

Slicing shrimp in half lengthwise for pizza is great for two reasons: it makes it easier to nestle the shrimp into the toppings and it helps to stretch an expensive ingredient. For the prettiest presentation, arrange the shrimp with the cut side down.

Place a pizza stone in the middle of the oven and preheat to 450°F (230°C). Once the oven has reached 450°F (230°C), let the stone continue to heat for 15–30 minutes longer, without opening the door.

On a floured pizza peel, stretch or roll out the pizza dough into 2 rounds about 12-inch (30-cm) each. If the dough springs back, let it rest for about 10 minutes before continuing. Leaving a 1-inch (2.5-cm) border, spread the red pepper sauce over the dough rounds and top with the cheese and 1 tablespoon of the oregano leaves.

In a bowl, toss the shrimp with the olive oil and season with salt and pepper. Chop the remaining 1 tablespoon oregano leaves and toss with the shrimp. Cover the pizza with the shrimp, cut side down. Brush the outside edge of the pizza with olive oil and season the pizza lightly with salt and pepper.

Carefully slide the pizza from the peel onto the hot stone in the oven and bake for 10–12 minutes, or until the shrimp are cooked through and the crust is golden brown. Using the peel, transfer the pizza to a cutting board. Let cool for a few minutes, then slice and serve right away.

SERVES 4

⅓ lb (155 g) andouille sausage, cut into ¼-inch (6-mm) slices

½ lb (250 g) medium shrimp, peeled, deveined, and halved lengthwise

2 teaspoons olive oil, plus more for brushing

Kosher salt and freshly ground pepper

1 ball Thin-Crust Pizza Dough (page 17) or Whole-Wheat Pizza Dough (page 20)

1 cup (8 fl oz/250 ml) Tomato Sauce (page 26)

1½ cups (6 oz/185 g) shredded fontina cheese

2 teaspoons fresh thyme leaves

ANDOUILLE, SHRIMP & FONTINA PIZZA

SURF & TURF PIZZA

>>>>>>>>

A generous shower of fresh thyme leaves adds an herbal element to the shrimp and andouille toppings. Elegant enough for entertaining, serve this pizza with your favorite Pinot Noir and Haricots Verts & Cherry Tomato Salad (page 116).

Place a pizza stone in the middle of the oven and preheat to 450°F (230°C). Once the oven has reached 450°F (230°C), let the stone continue to heat for 15–30 minutes longer, without opening the door.

In a frying pan over medium-high heat, fry the sausage slices until lightly browned on both sides, about 5 minutes. Using a slotted spoon, transfer to paper towels to drain.

In a bowl, toss the shrimp with the olive oil and season with salt and pepper. Set aside.

On a floured pizza peel, stretch or roll out the pizza dough into a 12-inch (30-cm) round. If the dough springs back, let it rest for about 10 minutes before continuing. Leaving a 1-inch (2.5-cm) border, spread the sauce over the dough round and top with the cheese. Distribute the sausage and the shrimp, cut side down, evenly around the pizza. Scatter the thyme all over the top. Brush the outside edge of the dough with olive oil and season the whole pizza lightly with salt and pepper.

Carefully slide the pizza from the peel onto the hot stone in the oven and bake for 10–12 minutes, or until the shrimp is opaque throughout and the crust is golden brown. Using the peel, transfer the pizza to a cutting board. Let cool for a few minutes, then slice and serve right away.

SERVES 4

WHAT YOU NEED

5 tablespoons (3 fl oz/80 ml) olive oil

3 cloves garlic, minced

1 cup (8 fl oz/250 ml) dry white wine or bottled clam juice

2½ lb (1.25 kg) littleneck clams, scrubbed and rinsed

1 ball Thin-Crust Pizza Dough (page 17)

1 teaspoon fennel seeds

¼ teaspoon red pepper flakes (optional)

Kosher salt and freshly ground black pepper

¾ cup (3 oz/90 g) grated pecorino romano cheese

4 oz (125 g) fresh mozzarella cheese, preferably buffalo, cut into ½-inch (12-mm) dice

WHITE CLAM PIZZA

Place a pizza stone in the middle of the oven and preheat to 450°F (230°C). Once the oven has reached 450°F (230°C), let the stone heat for 15–30 minutes longer, without opening the door.

In a large, heavy-bottomed saucepan over medium heat, warm 1 tablespoon of the olive oil. Add half of the garlic and sauté just until it softens, about 1 minute. Pour in the wine and bring to a gentle boil. Add the clams, discarding any that do not close to the touch. Cover the pan and cook, shaking the covered pot a few times, until the clams open, 6–8 minutes. Remove from the heat and let cool. Discard any clams that didn't open. When cool enough to handle, remove the clam meat from each shell and set aside.

On a floured pizza peel, stretch or roll out the pizza dough into a 12-inch (30-cm) round. If the dough springs back, let it rest for 10 minutes before continuing.

In a small frying pan over medium heat, warm 2 tablespoons of the olive oil. Add the remaining garlic, the fennel seeds, and red pepper flakes, if using. Sauté just until the garlic softens and the oil is fragrant, about 1 minute. Brush the dough all over with the flavored oil and season well with salt and black pepper. Top with the cheeses and clams. Drizzle with 1 tablespoon of the olive oil.

Carefully slide the pizza from the peel onto the hot stone in the oven and bake until the crust is golden brown, 10–12 minutes. Using the peel, transfer the pizza to a cutting board and drizzle with the remaining 1 tablespoon olive oil. Let cool for a few minutes, then slice and serve right away.

SERVES 4

CLAM UP YOUR PIZZA

While fresh clams are going to produce the best results for this pizza, you can use canned or frozen clams as well—look for whole-belly clams, rather than prechopped clams, which can get chewy once cooked.

2 boneless, skin-on chicken breast halves, about 1 lb (500 g) total

⅓ cup (3 fl oz/80 ml) olive oil, plus more for brushing

Kosher salt and freshly ground pepper

3 small cloves garlic

4 anchovy fillets

1 tablespoon fresh lemon juice

1 large egg yolk

1 teaspoon Worcestershire sauce

6 tablespoons (1½ oz/45 g) grated Parmesan cheese

2 hearts of romaine lettuce, cored and chopped

1 Thin-Crust Pizza Dough (page 17)

2 teaspoons fresh thyme leaves, chopped

CHICKEN CAESAR PIADINE

Preheat the oven to 375°F (190°C).

Pat the chicken dry and put it on a small baking sheet. Brush with 1 tablespoon olive oil and season with salt and pepper. Roast the chicken until opaque throughout, 20–25 minutes. Remove from the oven and let cool. When cool enough to handle, discard the skin and cut or shred the chicken into bite-sized pieces. Set aside.

Raise the oven temperature to 450°F (230°C) and place a pizza stone on the middle rack. Once the oven has reached 450°F (230°C), let the stone continue to heat for 15–30 minutes longer, without opening the door.

Put the garlic, anchovies, lemon juice, egg yolk, and Worcestershire sauce in a blender and process until smooth. With the motor running, add the ⅓ cup (3 fl oz/80 ml) olive oil in a steady stream and blend until well combined. Stop the machine, add 3 tablespoons of the Parmesan, and pulse to mix. Taste and adjust the seasoning. Set aside.

To make the piadine, divide the pizza dough into 4 equal pieces. On a floured pizza peel, roll out each piece into a 6-inch (15-cm) round. Brush the piadine with olive oil, sprinkle with the thyme, and season with salt and pepper. Carefully slide the piadines from the peel onto the hot stone in the oven and bake until golden brown, 4–6 minutes. Using the peel, remove from the oven, then transfer to individual plates.

While the piadine are baking, assemble the salad: In a large bowl, toss the lettuce with the Caesar dressing, the remaining 3 tablespoons Parmesan, and the chicken. Top each of the piadine with the chicken salad, dividing it evenly, and serve right away.

SERVES 4

A piadine is an Italian flatbread that makes the perfect base for any of the salads in this book. Simply pile the salad high on the piadine, pick it up like a taco, and enjoy! The Caesar salad used here also makes a terrific side for any of the pizzas. Mix things up by substituting grilled shrimp or flank steak for the chicken. Do not consume raw eggs if you have health and safety concerns. A pasteurized egg product can be used as a replacement.

EASY SIDES
& SALADS

2 tablespoons minced garlic

2 tablespoons minced shallot

5 tablespoons (3 oz/80 g) sour cream

¼ cup (2 fl oz/60 ml) buttermilk

2 tablespoons fresh lemon juice

2 teaspoons chopped fresh tarragon

Kosher salt and freshly ground pepper

1½ cups (9 oz/280 g) cherry tomatoes

1 cup (5 oz/155 g) hazelnuts, toasted

1 heart of romaine lettuce, cored and chopped

1 small head radicchio, cored and chopped

1 small cucumber, peeled and chopped

8 radishes, chopped

CHOPPED SALAD WITH TARRAGON-BUTTERMILK DRESSING

To make the dressing, in a bowl, combine the garlic, shallot, sour cream, buttermilk, lemon juice, tarragon, ½ teaspoon salt, and ¼ teaspoon pepper and whisk to blend well. Set aside.

Quarter the tomatoes and roughly chop the hazelnuts. In a large salad bowl, combine the lettuce, radicchio, cucumber, radishes, tomatoes, and hazelnuts and toss to mix. Pour in the dressing and toss to coat all the ingredients well. Taste and adjust the seasoning. Serve right away.

SERVES 6

A WINNING FORMULA

A chopped salad is simply a bunch of vegetables, greens, and other ingredients cut into uniform pieces and tossed in a big bowl with dressing. This easy formula is an ideal solution for using up leftovers. Here the recipe features all vegetables, and some nuts, but you could add cheese, salami, or shredded rotisserie chicken for a heartier salad.

6 tablespoons (3 fl oz/90 ml) extra-virgin olive oil

¼ cup (2 fl oz/60 ml) balsamic vinegar

1 red onion, cut into wedges

1 globe eggplant, cut into ½-inch (12-mm) slices

2–3 yellow bell peppers, left whole or seeded and cut into big chunks

2–4 squashes, such as zucchini or pattypan, left whole or cut on the diagonal into slices about ½ inch (12 mm) thick

1 bunch asparagus, trimmed

¼ cup (⅓ oz/10 g) fresh thyme leaves, chopped

Kosher salt and freshly ground pepper

GRILLED VEGETABLES WITH BALSAMIC VINEGAR & THYME

This dish is easy to vary through the seasons. In spring and summer, asparagus, leeks, mushrooms, squashes, sweet and hot peppers, eggplant, and portobello mushrooms make great choices. In the cooler months, swap in sweet potatoes, sliced hard-shelled squash, or broccolini. Too cold to grill? Use the marinade to roast the vegetables in the oven instead.

Build a medium-hot fire in a charcoal grill or preheat a gas grill to medium-high.

In a small bowl, whisk together the olive oil and balsamic vinegar. Arrange the onion, eggplant, peppers, squash, and asparagus on a baking sheet. Brush on all sides with the vinaigrette and season well with the thyme, salt, and pepper, tossing to coat.

Spray the grill rack with nonstick cooking spray. Working in batches, begin grilling the vegetables that take the longest to cook and move through the faster-cooking pieces, cooking each until fork-tender. The onion will take about 6 minutes per side; the peppers about 4 minutes per side; and the squash and asparagus will cook the fastest, about 3 minutes per side. Return the vegetables to the baking sheet as they're finished.

Arrange all of the vegetables on a platter and serve warm or at room temperature.

SERVES 4–6

1 clove garlic, minced

½ teaspoon Dijon mustard

2 tablespoon red wine vinegar

Kosher salt and freshly ground pepper

2 tablespoons extra-virgin olive oil

1 head romaine lettuce, cored and chopped

1 can (15 oz/470 g) Italian butter beans, rinsed and drained

2 oz (60 g) salami, thinly sliced and julienned

3 oz (90 g) thinly sliced provolone cheese

2 jarred roasted red peppers, drained and chopped

2 or 3 pickled peperoncini, seeded and sliced

ANTIPASTI SALAD

Here's an easy variation on the classic pizza parlor staple featuring sliced cheese, salami, and peperoncini tossed with salad greens. This recipe calls for the addition of roasted red peppers for sweetness and Italian butter beans for protein.

In a large salad bowl, combine the garlic, mustard, vinegar, and salt and pepper to taste. Pour in the olive oil slowly, whisking until well blended. Taste and adjust the seasoning.

Add the lettuce, beans, salami, cheese, roasted peppers, and peperoncini to the bowl. Toss to coat all the ingredients well with the vinaigrette. Serve right away.

SERVES 4–6

¼ cup (2 fl oz/60 ml) balsamic vinegar

8 oz (250 g) fresh mozzarella cheese, preferably buffalo, sliced, at room temperature

1 lb (500 g) ripe tomatoes, thickly sliced

1½ tablespoons extra-virgin olive oil

Kosher salt and freshly ground pepper

4–6 basil leaves

CAPRESE SALAD WITH BALSAMIC SYRUP

To make the balsamic syrup, pour the vinegar into a small, heavy-bottomed saucepan and place over high heat. Bring to a gentle boil, then reduce the heat to low and let the vinegar simmer gently until very thick, 6–8 minutes. Remove from the heat and let cool slightly. (If you let the syrup sit too long, it will harden. Simply return to a low heat to soften.)

On a serving platter, arrange the mozzarella and tomato slices, alternating them in rows or another pattern. Drizzle with the olive oil and balsamic syrup and season with salt and pepper. Scatter the basil over the top, tearing the leaves into smaller pieces as you do, and serve right away.

SERVES 4

This composed salad is best made with juicy tomatoes at the peak of ripeness. For added color contrast, use a combination of tomato colors and types, including heirlooms, grape, and cherry tomatoes. For an easy variation, drizzle with pesto or olive tapenade.

6 slices thick-cut bacon

3 tablespoons red wine vinegar

1½ teaspoons honey

1 teaspoon Dijon mustard

½ small red onion, thinly sliced

5 oz (155 g) baby spinach

1 pear, cored and thinly sliced

Freshly ground pepper

SPINACH, PEAR, RED ONION & BACON SALAD

In a frying pan over medium-high heat, fry the bacon until crisp, about 6 minutes. Transfer to paper towels to drain, reserving the fat in the pan. When the bacon is cool enough to handle, crumble or tear it into bite-size pieces. Set aside.

Spoon 3 tablespoons of the reserved bacon fat into a small saucepan and place over medium heat. Whisk in the vinegar, honey, and mustard and simmer for a minute or two, until slightly thickened. Stir in the onion slices and remove from the heat.

Pour the dressing into a large salad bowl and add the spinach, pear, and crumbled bacon. Toss to coat all the ingredients well. Top with a few grindings of pepper and serve right away.

SERVES 4

HEALTHY GREENS

Fresh spinach is full of nutrients and a welcome addition to the dinner table. This salty-and-sweet version uses ripe pear for even more nutrients and fiber. Go light on the seasoning, since the bacon adds ample saltiness to both the dressing and the tossed greens; a few grinds of fresh pepper should do it.

1 large butternut squash, about 1½–2 lb (750 g–1 kg), peeled, seeded, and cubed

6 tablespoons (3 fl oz/90 ml) extra-virgin olive oil

3 tablespoons brown sugar

Kosher salt and freshly ground pepper

5 oz (155 g) baby arugula

2 tablespoons fresh lemon juice

½ cup (2 oz/60 g) walnuts, toasted and broken into pieces

⅓ cup (1½ oz/45 g) dried cherries

SQUASH, DRIED CHERRY, WALNUT & ARUGULA SALAD

WINTER SALAD SOLUTION

>>>>>>>>>>

You can use any type of winter squash or even sweet potatoes in this comforting salad. You can also try hazelnuts or pecans instead of walnuts, or swap the dried cherries for pomegranate seeds.

Preheat the oven to 400°F (200°C).

Pile the cubed squash on a baking sheet lined with parchment paper. Drizzle with 3 tablespoons of the olive oil, sprinkle with the brown sugar, and season well with salt and pepper. Toss to coat, then spread out the squash in a single layer. Roast, stirring once about halfway through, until caramelized and fork tender, 20–25 minutes. Set aside and let cool.

In a large salad bowl, toss the arugula with the remaining 3 tablespoons olive oil, the lemon juice, and salt and pepper to taste. Add the butternut squash, walnuts, and dried cherries and toss gently to combine. Serve right away.

SERVES 4

1 medium shallot, minced

1½ teaspoons Dijon mustard

1 tablespoon red wine vinegar

Kosher salt and freshly ground pepper

2 tablespoons extra-virgin olive oil

Kosher salt and freshly ground pepper

8 oz (250 g) haricots verts, trimmed

1 cup (6 oz/185 g) cherry tomatoes, halved

HARICOTS VERTS & CHERRY TOMATO SALAD

VEGETABLES MADE EASY

Make sure to toss the beans in the dressing while they are still warm so they absorb more of the dressing's flavor. You can also use regular green beans for this simple salad; just increase the cooking time to 3 minutes.

Bring a small saucepan of water to a boil over medium-high heat.

Meanwhile, make the vinaigrette: In a large salad bowl, combine the shallot, mustard, vinegar, and salt and pepper to taste. Pour in the olive oil, whisking until well blended. Taste and adjust the seasoning. Set aside.

Stir ½ teaspoon salt into the boiling water, then add the beans and cook until al dente, about 2 minutes. Drain but do not rinse.

Add the haricots verts and tomato halves to the bowl with the vinaigrette and toss well to make sure each bean and tomato is nicely coated.

Serve warm, at room temperature, or chilled.

SERVES 4

---

1 teaspoon Dijon mustard

3 tablespoons fresh lemon juice

Finely grated zest of 1 lemon

Kosher salt and freshly ground pepper

¼ cup (2 fl oz/60 ml) extra-virgin olive oil

½ small red onion, thinly sliced

1 can (15 oz/470 g) chickpeas, rinsed and drained

1 large bunch kale

¼ lb ricotta salata, shaved or cut into small chunks, or crumbled feta cheese

KALE, CHICKPEA & RICOTTA SALATA SALAD

In the bottom of a large salad bowl, combine the mustard, lemon juice and zest, and salt and pepper to taste. Pour in the olive oil slowly, whisking until well blended. Taste and adjust the seasoning. Add the onion and chickpeas to the dressing and toss to mix.

Remove the stems and tough center spines from the kale and roughly chop the leaves. Add the kale and cheese to the bowl and toss to mix well and coat all of the ingredients with the dressing. Serve right away.

SERVES 4–6

KALE FOR GOOD HEALTH

Loaded with vitamins A, K, and C and packed with iron, it's hard to beat the nutritional powerhouse that is kale, so it's an excellent addition to a midweek family meal. This salad is a great accompaniment to any pizza, but especially some of the spicy meat-topped pizzas.

2 zucchini

2 tablespoons olive oil

1 tablespoon fresh lemon juice

6 fresh mint leaves, chopped

Kosher salt and freshly ground pepper

3 oz (90 g) Parmesan cheese, shaved

2 tablespoons pine nuts, toasted (optional)

ZUCCHINI RIBBONS WITH PARMESAN, LEMON & MINT

Using a mandoline or a vegetable peeler, shave each zucchini into long, very thin ribbons. Transfer to a large bowl. Add the olive oil, lemon juice, and mint and toss to mix. Season to taste with salt and pepper.

Transfer the salad to a serving platter and garnish with the Parmesan shavings. Sprinkle the pine nuts all over the top, if using. Serve at once.

SERVES 4

SLICE IT THIN

The easiest way to make ribbons from a zucchini is with a mandoline. But you can also use a wide vegetable peeler or a very sharp knife to cut thin ribbons. The trick is to use zucchini at the height of it's season and to get the pieces as thin as possible since you aren't cooking the vegetable. For a pretty presentation, try using half zucchini and half yellow squash.

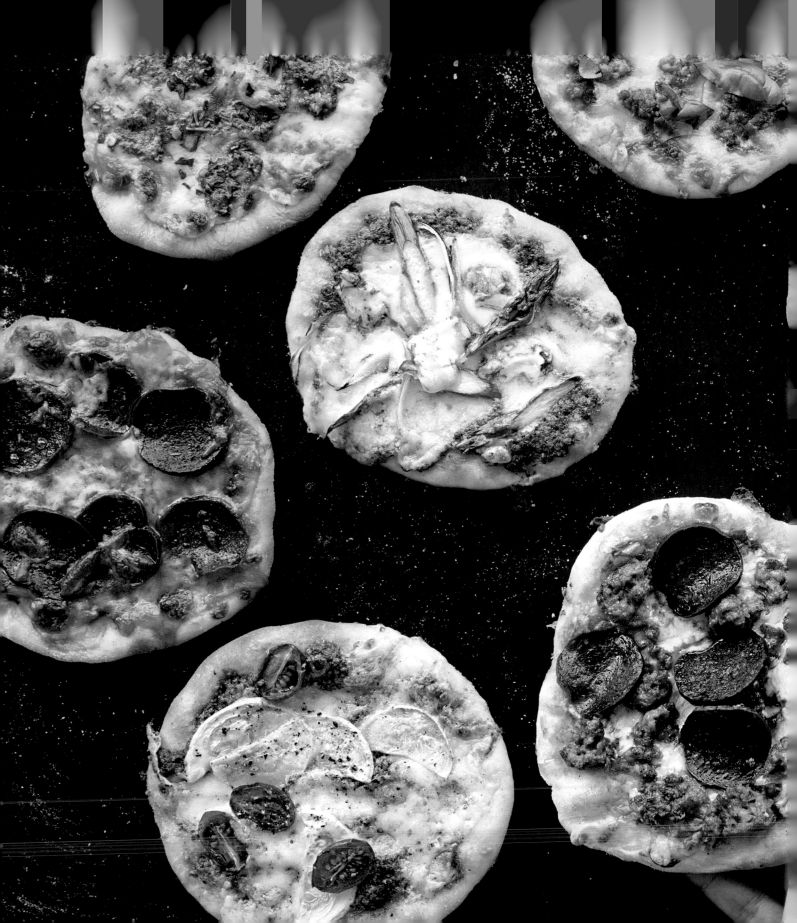

MENUS

From busy weeknights with kids to entertaining guests on a Saturday, planning a delicious, balanced dinner is a cinch with these menus as your guide. For tips on planning a dinner timeline see page 12.

MANIC MONDAY

Pull out the pre-made frozen sauce and dough to thaw on Sunday for an effortless, homemade dinner Monday.

MARGHERITA PIZZA (page 38)

FOUR CHEESE PIZZA (page 48)

CAPRESE SALAD WITH BALSAMIC SYRUP (page 111)

FOR THE ADULTS White wine

FOR THE KIDS Shirley Temples

HEALTHY

Pizza night gets a healthy makeover with the addition of nutritious vegetable toppings and a hearty side salad.

BROCCOLI RABE, GARLIC & SMOKED MOZZERELLA PIZZA (page 47)

ARTICHOKE, SPINACH & OLIVE TAPENADE PIZZA (page 42)

KALE, CHICKPEA & RICOTTA SALATA SALAD (page 117)

FOR THE KIDS & ADULTS Seltzer with lemons and limes

ROMANTIC NIGHT-IN

An elegant pizza and a bottle of chilled wine is just the ticket for date night.

GRILLED PIZZA WITH MOZZARELLA, PROSCIUTTO & PEACHES (page 97)

CHOPPED SALAD (page 107)

FOR THE ADULTS Chilled rosé

"KID-FRIENDLY"

Kids can have fun topping pizzettes (mini pizzas) with their favorite toppings for an adult to bake and slice.

1 BALL THIN CRUST PIZZA (PAGE 17), SHAPED INTO MINI PIZZETTES + YOUR FAVORITE TOPPINGS

FOR THE ADULTS Crisp white wine

FOR THE KIDS Sparkling lemonade

MEAT LOVER

Fulfill a meat-lover's dream with this pork- and beef-studded meal.

MINI MEATBALL & RED ONION PIZZA (page 62)

GROUND BEEF, GREEN OLIVE & ASIAGO PIZZA (page 67)

ANTIPASTI SALAD (page 110)

FOR THE ADULTS Your favorite beer

FOR THE KIDS Root beer soda

BRUNCH

With toppings like smoked salmon and eggs, there's no reason pizza can't become a brunch staple.

SMOKED SALMON PIZZETTES (page 89)

SHAVED ASPARAGUS & HERB PIZZA WITH EGG (page 37)

FOR THE ADULTS Mimosas

FOR THE KIDS Fresh-squeezed OJ

INDEX